ARNOLD VAN GENNEP

NICOLE BELMONT

Arnold Van Gennep

*The Creator of
French Ethnography*

Translated by Derek Coltman

The University of Chicago Press
Chicago and London

Nicole Belmont is maître-assistant at the
Ecole des Hautes Etudes en sciences sociales,
Paris. Since 1960 she has worked in association
with Claude Lévi-Strauss in the Laboratoire
d'anthropologie sociale. Her published works include
*Les Signes de la naissance: Etude des représentations
symboliques associées aux naissances singulières*
and *Mythes et croyances dans l'ancienne France*, and she
is the editor of *A. Van Gennep: Textes inédits*.

This book first appeared in French
under the title *Arnold Van Gennep:
Le créateur de l'ethnographie française*.
Copyright © Payot, Paris, 1974

The University of Chicago Press, Chicago 60637
The University of Chicago Press, Ltd., London

Library of Congress Cataloging in Publication Data

Belmont, Nicole.
    Arnold Van Gennep: the creator of French ethnography.

    Translation of Arnold Van Gennep: créateur de
l'ethnographie française.
    Bibliography: p.
    1. Gennep, Arnold Van, 1873–1957.   I. Title.
GN21.G46B4413   301.2'092'4   78–8680
ISBN 0–226–04216–2

CONTENTS

v

Contents

ONE

INTRODUCTION

How does one become a folklorist? If we are to take the case of Arnold Van Gennep as typical, then the path toward folklore is at once tortuous yet logical. Tortuous, because in his case it wound via numismatology, Egyptology, a study of Arabic and Islamic culture, the religious sciences, and, finally, classical ethnology. Logical, because all these apparently disparate disciplines helped lead him, to a greater or lesser degree, toward his final goal.

Even before he had completed his secondary education, as we know from Van Gennep himself, he had already become fascinated, not only by the old coins he had begun to collect in Savoy, but also by the prehistory of that region, particularly that of the lakeside civilizations. At the very beginning of his scientific career, therefore, we find both deep geographical roots and a very lively appreciation of material objects and the concrete. Yet he was born not in Savoy but in Germany, at Ludwigsburg, in 1873, where he remained until his sixth year. It was only later that chance and family circumstances led him to Savoy.[1]

When he arrived in Paris in order to complete his higher
education, he found that the Sorbonne did not provide the
kind of program he was looking for. As a consequence he
applied to the Ecole des langues orientales for instruction
in Arabic, to the Historical Sciences department of the
Ecole pratique des hautes études for enrollment in its
philology, general linguistics, Egyptology, and Ancient
Arabic courses, and to the same institution's Religious
Studies department for courses in primitive religions and
Islamic culture. This independent attitude toward the
official university establishment became even more
pronounced as his scientific career developed: Van Gennep never occupied any academic post in France and
remained all his life outside the French university hierar-
chy. As far as the years before the 1914–18 war are concerned, Van Gennep summarizes the situation himself in
his unpublished notes (see note 3, below) for the conclusion to his *Manuel de folklore français contemporain*: after 1890

> there grew up a fairly violent antagonism between all
> the sciences of man constituted in previous years as
> a result of the revival of Comtist sociology instigated
> by Durkheim. The latter drew his support from the
> teaching staff of the universities, while his opponents
> had their headquarters in the Collège de France and
> the Institut de France. Closing ranks, the Durkheimists
> instituted a siege of these positions and within about
> twenty years successfully reduced them to subjection.
> Anyone who was not a member of their group was a
> "marked man."

And Van Gennep himself was of course not a member. In
fact, as we shall see, he expressed fairly violent opposition
to Durkheim and the entire French sociological school,
who in return treated him with at best indifference and at

worst hostility. On the other hand, Van Gennep was also establishing good relations during these apprentice years with a fair number of fascinating and independent thinkers. Among the older generation there were Henri Maspéro, the Egyptologist; Michel Bréal, the linguist; Henri Gaidoz, who taught Celtic language and literature at the Ecole pratique des hautes études and was the founder of the *Revue Celtique* and *Mélusine*; Derenbourg, an Arabist and professor of Classical Arabic at the Ecole des langues orientales; Jean Réville, a lecturer at the Ecole pratique des hautes études specializing in the history of religions; and Léon Marillier, who occupied the chair of primitive religions in the same establishment.[2] Among his fellow students we find A. Meillet, W. Marsais, a specialist in Islamic civilization, and G. Jéquier. He also knew J. Deniker, the specialist in race studies, the folklorist Paul Sébillot, the numismatologists Babelon and Prou, and Joseph Bédier the specialist in medieval literature.

Having broken off relations with his family when they refused to approve of his marriage to a young woman without a dowry, Van Gennep then accepted a post teaching French in Poland, where he remained for four years. This interlude enabled him to add Polish to the already long list of languages he had acquired and also, with the aid of philology, a number of other Slavic languages, including Russian. He had in fact spoken four languages—French, German, English, and Spanish—from childhood and had also learned Italian during his years at high school in Nice and Chambéry. He was only too well aware of the tremendous advantage conferred by a knowledge of a great many languages. He had always shown an interest in linguistics, even though that interest never extended outside the strict limits of the relation between linguistics and ethnography. Numerous articles in the five

volumes of *Religions, moeurs et légendes* bear witness to this
(see the Bibliography, below). One of these in particular
shows his very acute understanding of language's social
role ("Internationalisme et particularisme linguistique,"
Religions, moeurs et légendes, vol. 1, pp. 308–16). In it he
attacks the utopian notion of international languages and
expresses his opinion that the world as a whole will evolve
in the direction of polyglotism, which will have become
inevitable and widespread by about the year 2000. For
example,

> every child will learn one Romance, one Germanic, one
> Slavic, one Semitic, one Mongol, and one Bantu lan-
> guage, with varying degrees of ease, but all helped by
> improved teaching methods and the application of ex-
> perimental phonetics. . . . [Children] will be taught suf-
> ficient linguistics for them to be able to progress easily,
> by applying known laws, from the selected language in
> any group to all the other languages in that group. . . .
> All argument, all propaganda on behalf of an interna-
> tional language, whether artificial or already existing, is
> worse than a throwback to the nineteenth century or
> ignorant simplemindedness: it is in fact an attempt to
> impede mankind's progress toward a greater richness
> and variety of intellectual production (pp. 315–16).

Sadly, we do not seem to be progressing at the moment
toward the cultural richness and diversity that Van Gennep desired, though this does not diminish the originality
of his most remarkable understanding of the roles and effects of social particularisms, and it is a theme that was to
reappear frequently in his work in a variety of contexts.
    When he returned to Paris, in 1901, his far-ranging
linguistic abilities earned him a position as head of the
translation department in the Ministry of Agriculture's
information office. He gave up this post in 1908, by which

time he was able to support himself on the income he
earned from his free-lance work: regular articles in the
Mercure de France, contributions to a variety of periodicals, plus lecturing and translating. He was to preserve
this total resistance to the lures of the French establishment, and of the universities in particular, throughout
his life, apart from a few brief exceptions: during the
1914–18 war he was recalled by Poincaré to a post in the
Foreign Office, where he remained until 1922. And although he did occupy a chair of ethnography for three
years, from 1912 to 1915, it was in Switzerland, at the
University of Neuchâtel. He also reorganized the museum there, and it was thanks to him that the first ethnographical congress was held in 1914. Having regained
his independence in 1922, in order to make a tour of
the United States, lecturing on French folk song and
country crafts, he then resumed the free-lance assignments
that enabled him to subsist, as well as work on personal
projects closer to his heart. It was not until after 1945, by
which time he was over seventy-two years old, that the
French Center for Scientific Research awarded him the
grant that enabled him to devote all his energies to his
Manuel de folklore français contemporain, which unfortunately
remained uncompleted at the time of his death in 1957.[3]

Even before he went to study in Paris, however, Van
Gennep was already possessed by the mania for research
that, up until his twentieth year, had found an outlet in the
collecting of "old pennies," bones, fibulas, and pottery and
in "fishing for prehistory" in the waters of the Lac du
Bourget.

These two passions, for coins and prehistory, brought
a double benefit: not only did they teach me how to
draw up a bibliography unaided, how to establish a
meticulous classification of my finds, based on minor

characteristics, and how to deal with source material; they also brought me into contact with a great variety of people, not only in cities and villages but also in the very depths of the countryside (*Titres et travaux*, p. 10).

He was in fact acquiring the very virtues that are indispensable to a good ethnologist. We shall see later how his coin-collecting led him to the purely ethnographic problem of property marks and brands, which occupied him at a very early stage and for a long time, despite the fact that it unfortunately never resulted in a comprehensive work on the subject. He had observed resemblances between Pyrenean property marks and certain signs to be found on Celtiberian coins, and this led him to formulate a hypothesis concerning the origin of alphabets (see below, pp. 103–5).

It was only during his vacations in Savoy that he was able to indulge this passion for collecting his "old pennies," since during the school term he was always in Nice, where he remained as either a day student or full boarder at the high school throughout his secondary education. He describes himself at this time as independent and insolent, working only in volcanic bursts and spending the remainder of his time lying in the sun, learning to throw a knife, or initiating himself into the intricacies of the local dialect. It was in Nice too, and in the countryside around it, which in those days was still as wild as Corsica, that he acquired his taste for friendly contact with people from every conceivable walk of life.

In this way I made useful friendships: I mean that I was able to wander along by the Paillon instead of attending classes, spend hours out at sea with the fishermen while they sang their sad, tuneless laments, hobnob by special dispensation with the smugglers in Beaulieu, and also, during the school walks to Villefranche on

Thursdays and Sundays, vanish suddenly at a bend in the path with a few close chums, scramble down the cliff, and visit certain disreputable open-air bars, where we were able to enjoy the favors of welcoming girls, American cigarettes, and a few glasses of white wine. Then later, when the time came for the more law-abiding pupils' immutable return along the Corniche, we made sure we were already concealed at the right time and place to make an unobserved reentry into the procession. The assistant masters in charge, as though aware of what was going on, always refrained from calling the roll until we were well back within the outskirts of town, except for one, who got us into trouble so often that there eventually came a night when we very carefully roped him between two mattresses and hurled him out of a first-floor window (*En Algérie*, pp. 122–23).

There is no doubt that Van Gennep's quite prodigious gift for languages also helped to foster his aptitude for ethnology. He himself said that it made comparative work much easier. In an article written in 1927 about the use of the subconscious in the study of living languages ("De l'utilisation du subconscient dans l'étude des langues vivantes," *La Psychologie et la vie* 1 no. 3 [May 1927]: 9–13) he admits to knowing eighteen languages plus a number of their dialects. This brief, seemingly uncontroversial article, published in the Institut Pelman magazine, to which he was a regular contributor for a number of years, ought to be more widely known. It is not really a methodological study but rather an account of various "tricks of the trade" for learning a language. The first rule, he writes, is to put oneself in a situation that will enable one to hear the language spoken over long periods of time in many different accents. This trains the ear, in much the same way as a musician has to train his. But one should always stop before saturation and fatigue set in. At the same time, one should exercise one's muscles in trying to imitate sounds, intonations, and even complete sentences. This physical training program, as it were, encourages automatic responses and flexibility. Next, one's method of learning the grammar should be the reverse of that usually employed. In other words, it is best to begin with the absolutely invariable elements and then progress to the variable ones. For instance, one should begin by learning invariable words, such as interjections, conjunctions, prepositions, and adverbs. Once mastered, they enable one to organize one's sentences, because one knows they are not going to change. Next, taking the roots of the adverbs as a starting point, one can progress to verbs, nouns, and adjectives. The one mistake to avoid is attempting to learn such words by their meanings. If you learn them by their roots, then any word summoned into one's consciousness by a text or a conversation brings with it the whole linguistic cluster to which it belongs. Another rule Van Gennep lays down, an extremely general one, is the importance of never trying to force the memory: deliberate repetition is useful, but it should never extend to the use of violent or exaggerated effort, since the invariable effect of that is to produce, not recall, but its contrary: inhibition. Anyone accustomed to using a foreign language is only too familiar with those notorious "black holes" of memory, words we know we know but that always vanish the moment we want to use them.

These rules appear to be no more than tricks of the trade, as I said earlier—of use when one wants to learn a new language, certainly, but without any general theoretical value. And yet, if we transpose these ideas from a language-learning situation to the situation of the ethnographer, embarking on a fieldwork project, then we can immediately discern more than one analogy between the two. In both cases what is involved is an attempt to discover meaning in things at present completely without meaning, whether sequences of sounds or letters, on the one hand, or observed actions, on the other. If we accept this analogy between the two situations, then one of Van Gennep's general rules may appear surprising: that of never learning anything by its meaning. On the other hand, the rule of placing oneself in a "bath" of strange sounds applies exactly to the situation of the ethnographer totally surrounded by the people he has just come to study. And although ethnographers are well aware of this situation, they do not always react in the way Van Gennep advocates: by establishing a happy balance within themselves between passivity and constraint, without ever forcing their will to learn, which tends to induce an inhibitory mechanism. The rule of learning a language's invariable elements first is also applicable to the ethnographer. For example, seeing the same gestures repeated in a variety of ceremonies will enable him to establish fixed points and connecting links. It is in this way, moving from social invariables to variables—which are never absolutely so in fact, since there are always rules governing them—that ethnographers gradually work toward a comprehension of what they are observing.

Returning to the problem of meaning, clearly the terms in which Van Gennep presents it contain a paradox. We must learn the vocabulary not by the meanings of the words but by their roots, he tells us. Transposed into ethnographical terms, this proposition might be expressed as follows: we should acquire our knowledge of practices, customs, beliefs—in a word, of the social system as a whole—not through their meaning but through the interconnecting relations that link them and make it possible to organize them into various subsystems. However paradoxical on the surface, this procedure is in fact a logical one. Experience shows that we do not really begin to know a language until the point is reached when we no longer need to make mental translation from or into our mother tongue. This is even more true in the case of ethnography, since no sociocultural system is, properly speaking, translatable into any other. Yet certain of their elements are, if not translatable, at least comparable: these are the elements we can isolate by means of formal analysis, notably in the case of kinship. It was by using an analogous method that Van Gennep was later to arrive at the notion of the rite of passage, or transition ritual (see below, p. 58), which he saw as a "schema" or blueprint making it possible to organize the chaotic multiplicity of ritual practices: "It is not the rites in their detail that interest us but rather...their relative situations within ceremonial wholes" (*Rites de passage*, p. 275).

This does not mean that Van Gennep was already a structuralist before his time. Always a weak theoretician, he was incapable of conceptualizing sufficiently what he perceived intuitively, so that he literally lived the relations between linguistics and ethnography without ever being able to state them theoretically. In the scientific context of his time it was not yet possible for linguistics to play midwife to a structuralist social anthropology.

Psychologically, the constant use of a great many languages can be of great benefit to the ethnologist, in the sense that it enables him to acquire great mental agility and flexibility in the manipulation of linguistic signs in their double, Saussurian, nature as signifiers and signifieds. This enables him to achieve a concrete understanding of the fact that "foreign" languages function in accordance with models (phonetic, syntactic, semantic) different from those of his mother tongue. Then, as a result of the mental shift that this realization automatically triggers, he is in a position to grasp the fact that societies, too, function in accordance with a variety of models, none of which is superior to the others. The mother tongue, or the society in which one was born, ceases to be the archetype or touchstone for all other language and societies. In these matters the sense of relativity, once acquired, provides access to a fuller understanding, because one has ceased to regard the "other" as foreign or a challenge.

This gift for languages aside, there was another factor, albeit a negative one, that contributed positively to Van Gennep's ethnographical training. French universities did not teach ethnology in those days, and indeed such a course was not to be offered at the Sorbonne until the appointment of Marcel Griaule in 1943. All students desiring a grounding in the subject therefore had to acquire it through the teaching of Durkheim and the French sociological school. Whether for good or for ill, this state of affairs probably had a great bearing on the later development of French ethnology. We have seen that Van Gennep deliberately elected to attend courses outside the university. This had the advantage of fueling his superabundant scientific curiosity with a great variety of disciplines; but it also presented the disadvantage of placing him outside the university "cycle of reproduction," which ensures that each generation of university teachers is always training up another to succeed it, thus forming an unbroken chain. Van Gennep did in fact apply for a chair of "ethnography and the history of religions" at the Collège de France, but his request came to nothing, and it was Switzerland that offered him his revenge. In 1912 the University of Neuchâtel created the first Swiss chair of ethnography at the instance of the Borel brothers, who provided funds for the venture. It was Henri Junod, a missionary and Bantu

specialist, who was appointed as its first incumbent. He
then stood down in favor of Van Gennep, who occupied
the post until 1915. The cause of his departure was political
in nature: he was in fact expelled from the country by the
federal government because he had written letters to the
Dépêche de Toulouse casting doubt on Swiss neutrality on
the basis of evidence he had received that it was being
violated by Swiss germanophiles (K. Van Gennep, *Bibliographie des oeuvres . . .*, p. 7). This was one more example—
a particularly striking one—of the independence of mind
he displayed throughout his life in refusing to swear allegiance to any one school or fashionable current of thought.
It was an independence for which he paid a high price,
moreover, since he was obliged almost throughout his life
to keep himself afloat financially with bread-and-butter
work: articles, reviews, translations, lectures, and so on.
However, even though the French university establishment kept him at arm's length, that does not mean that he
lived in isolation. For one thing, he was in constant touch
with the large circle of correspondents he had acquired as a
result of the folklore questionnaires he sent out to the
various French regions. And we have already noted the
connections he made during his student years with a considerable number of his teachers and fellow students. In
1908 he founded a periodical called *Revue des Etudes ethno-
graphiques et sociologiques* which later, in 1910, became the
Revue d'ethnographie et de sociologie and continued to appear
under that name until 1914. He was also, until 1940, a
regular contributor to the *Mercure de France*, for which he
acted as regular correspondent in the fields of ethnography, folklore, prehistory, anthropology, and the history
of religions. We have seen, too, that between 1927 and
1933, approximately, he did work for the Institut Pelman
and contributed many articles to its magazine, *La*

Psychologie et la vie. Such a ferment of intellectual and literary activity hardly accords with the image of a man locked up in an ivory tower. He found it easy to talk to anyone and everyone, irrespective of social class, probably because it never occurred to him to draw any dividing line between the science he was striving to guide along the right road and his own personal existence. We can see two reasons for this. First, the aim of ethnography, the science to which he devoted his whole life (or at least from his twenty-third year onward, as he himself tells us), is precisely that of acquiring an understanding of other men. As we read him, we sense that he truly lived ethnography the same way one lives one's personal existence. In an article written in 1907 (now in *Religions, moeurs et légendes,* 2:239), mainly an account of the results of certain investigations he had been making in Haute-Savoie, he attempts to convey the fascination exerted by his subject:

> The greatest charm of ethnography is, perhaps, that once its simplest rudiments have been acquired and its specific method grasped, one's daily life takes on a new aspect. Some trifling isolated fact, or some chance remark overheard in passing, because one perceives its links with an entire network of beliefs and customs, can conjure up a whole world of analogies and memories.

Transposed into the field of science, it is a veritably Proustian universe that Van Gennep is evoking there. In his unpublished notes he expresses this inner identification even more clearly:

> A certain reticence prevents the scientist from displaying the feeling he puts into his work, a reticence imposed on him by indoctrination, by fashion, and often by a belief in himself as a creature existing above all passions. I do not feel this reticence myself, partly, I

suppose, because my temperament happens to run
quite counter to it, but also because I have spent time
with other men who, in my presence at least, did not
feel it either: Maspéro and Oppert, Curie and Kropot-
kin, Matruchot and Bohn, Havelock Ellis and Wester-
marck, Philippe and René Berthelot, Léon Brunschvicg
and Meillet, Rivet and Sébillot, and a number of others
in other fields, poets, painters, sculptors, musicians.

As early as 1914, with reference to Frazer's *Golden Bough*
but also to his own *Rites de passage*, he wrote:

a book dealing with general theory, even when couched
in superficially cool language, expresses intense mental
turbulence. I believe, in fact, that although the collecting of facts may leave one calm and serene in brain and
body, the slightest attempt at theory, even on a tiny
point of detail, excites the deepest fibers of the being.
Hence the frequent bitterness of theoretical polemics. It
is as if the theoretician's very life depended—to a
greater or lesser degree, varying with individual
temperament—upon his colleagues' acceptance of the
theory being proposed (*Religions, moeurs et légendes*,
5:40).

This intimate, familiar bond between the scientist and
his science, an identification experienced at every waking
moment, is another aspect of the gift for observation so
essential to the ethnologist, a gift that Van Gennep himself
possessed in the highest degree. To him, everything was
grist to the mill of science, down to the minutest facts of
everyday life, because he had the power to discern the
unexpected beneath the mundane in everything: he lived
in the midst of his own society like an ethnographer observing some remote tribe. In his eyes, this gift was the
very antithesis of erudition, and in his little book *Le Folklore*
he makes his explanation of this antithesis an opportunity
to aim a few darts at history in passing:

This observation . . . explains why historians have for a
long time scorned folklore and why the best folklorists
of the past century were naturalists, geologists,
biologists, painters, artists in general, or at least scientists who possessed a gift for firsthand observation as
well as the gift that characterizes the learned academic.
The supremacy accorded to history over the natural sciences during the nineteenth century, in other words,
that of erudition over the direct observation of natural
phenomena—despite the high regard such observation
enjoyed in the eighteenth century—also explains the archeological mania that is such an obstacle to the progress of our science (p. 34).

This passage is interesting on several counts. First, there is
the tartness of Van Gennep's tone when referring to history. We shall return later (p. 113, below) to the problem of
the relations between folklore and history, which for him
were relations of exclusion, and we shall find that things
are not quite so simple as he would have had them. Another of Van Gennep's dominant ideas also appears here:
that ethnography is a biological science because it studies
living facts in their environment (in the same way as zool-
ogy and botany). In other words, ethnography belongs to
the natural sciences because man is part of nature (see
Appendix, "Nature and Sexuality"). In a 1934 article,
"Contribution à la méthodologie du folklore," in which he
followed his usual habit of interspersing his scientific
material with personal confidences, he examines the origin
of his taste for biology and the way in which that science
has affected his methodological thinking:

you should know that my father, a well-known laryn-
gologist, had me making up microscope slides from the
age of fifteen, since it was his hope that I would succeed him in his practice at Challes-les-Eaux. And a Pas-
teurian training stays with one for life. Then I fell in

love with biology; but gradually human biology came
to fascinate me more than that of plants or animals. Despite myself, I applied to ethnography and folklore the
great biological method whose "gods" in France are
Claude Bernard, Pasteur, and Giard. I took to approaching the facts of civilization from a biological
angle, to examining all its manifestations, however
primitive or highly evolved, in accordance with the
methods of embryogeny and the comparative natural
sciences, and this meant that I was innocently setting
myself in opposition to the historical method on the one
hand and to the official sociological method on the
other. I was consequently regarded for a long time as a
pariah, even though I had also assimilated the two latter methods as well, as any French person must who
has been through high school and a university Arts
faculty. But when one is faced with the facts, then all
labels lose their value, except for the label "Biology."
For we ethnographers and folklorists are dealing with
living facts, and therefore with facts in a perpetual state
of transformation whose constants—if not their variants
too—are governed by cosmic laws (p. 25).

These passages are best read in conjunction with one written in 1911 (appearing in the Appendix, below, as "What Is
Ethnography?"), not only because then the remarkable
coherence in Van Gennep's thought throughout his work
becomes apparent, but also because of the light that each
throws on the other. In the extract "What Is Ethnography?" he asserts in fact that it is the business of ethnography to study the factors and modalities of the genesis of
human activities; it is an introduction to the general science of civilizations, hence the importance of using the
biological and embryogenic methods.

In the passage quoted above (p. 15) from his book *Le
Folklore* we also find a partial answer to the question: How

does one become a folklorist? In the nineteenth century, at least, one became a good folklorist if one had not trained for it, if one possessed a training in the natural sciences or artistic gifts that provided one with direct access to living facts. This was not exactly the curriculum that Van Gennep himself had followed, but we have seen that he did in fact avoid subjecting himself to the one course of indoctrination into social facts then available (in other words sociology, since at that time no courses in ethnology, let alone folklore, even existed). What he did do was to take courses in a great number of related subjects, so that he was able to stalk and surround his main subject of study, as it were, before gradually closing in on it, thereby avoiding the risk of one day failing to see the wood for the trees.

He was thus an amateur, in the sense that his education had not specifically prepared him for his later research; in the sense that his scientific activities were not professional; and above all in the primary and strongest sense of the word: because he loved ethnography and folklore and because they were inseparable from his very existence. In the book he wrote about the months he spent in Algeria, in 1911 and then again in 1912, he confesses: "Research in the fields of ethnography and folklore is by now no longer a labor or a profession or a pastime with me: it is an organic necessity to which I must yield on pain of becoming, if not ill, at least ill at ease in my normal life" (*En Algérie*, pp. 125–26).

Ethnography, folklore: Van Gennep seems to make very little distinction between the terms. And indeed, for him they formed a single discipline dealing with collective, living facts. It was simply that scientific tradition had allotted non-Indo-European populations to ethnography and the rural populations of Europe to folklore. Van Gennep accepted this traditional terminology without fuss: all his regional monographs dealing with France include the word folklore in their titles (*Le Folklore du Dauphiné, Le Folklore de la Bourgogne, Le Folklore de la Flandres et du Hainaut français,* and so on). Similarly, his vast general work on the subject is entitled: *Manuel de folklore français contemporain*. But he refuses absolutely to let this traditional terminology conceal another distinction. The fact was that in those days folklore was taken by all the relevant specialists to be simply a matter of survivals, vestiges, and archaisms. For Van Gennep, on the contrary, "the ethnography of European rural populations" (alias folklore) is concerned with *living* collective facts. Indeed, as we shall see, it ought also to be applied, in his view, to "nascent facts," and it was a manual of *contemporary* French folklore that was to constitute his last—and, alas, unfinished—major work. He was extremely vehement in his attacks on those nineteenth- and early twentieth-century folklorists, the antiquarians of the social sciences, who collected quaint customs, stories handed down from generation to generation, or medical recipes based on spells and simples, rather as one might collect pressed, dried flowers as a hobby. It must be admitted, however, that he was kicking against the facts, since there has always been, and still is, a very real link between folklore and archaism. Michel Leiris has given us a very good account of this folkloric "ideology":

By definition, those social facts that fall into the realm of folklore present an old-fangled appearance, relatively and in practice at least. Those that receive most attention are the most picturesque, those that immediately catch the eye because of the oddity conferred on them by their archaism, itself often heightened by an element of exoticism. Moreover, this exoticism is not dependent on importation from another country. It may derive merely from a disparity between two environments: the

country can seem exotic when seen from the city, for
example, the provinces as seen from the capital, or even
working-class culture when seen through middle-class
eyes, which have a tendency to regard as at least
implicitly folkloric certain ways and customs of the
working class that appear to them as naive or anti-
quated (linked with long-dead fashions) in relation to
their own ways and customs. They will thus tend to see
the custom of clinking glasses, for example, as belonging to the realm of folklore, but not the ritual involved
in drinking a toast.[4]

Posed in such extreme terms, the dispute becomes in-
soluble, since the partisans of living folklore will never find
any ground for agreement with the students of survivals.
The solution to this radical antithesis lies elsewhere. It is
hinted at by Michel Leiris himself, in the work just quoted.
He points out that in fact, if one attempts to preserve the
manifestations of folklore "simply for preservation's sake,"
then the end result is merely empty, artificial, academic
forms, whereas those folklore phenomena that manage to
subsist without external intervention, even if they may appear archaic on the surface, are responding to a necessity
and fulfilling a function. Lévi-Strauss expressed this ad-
mirably with reference to our Christmas rituals: "Explanations by survival are always incomplete, because customs
do not vanish or survive without reason. When they
survive, the reason is to be found less in the viscosity of the
historic process than in the durability of a function that
analysis of the present should make it possible to discern."[5] Van Gennep would have subscribed to those
words, wishing as he did to explain the past by the present
and to reveal in present-day ways and customs not only
the submerged beliefs of yesterday but also the seeds of
beliefs to come.

Retaining the traditional terminology, then, Van

Gennep occupied himself mainly with ethnography during
the early part of his life and with French folklore during
the latter part of it. And we can locate the dividing line between the two periods in about 1924, the year he published
his short book entitled *Le Folklore*. But whereas during the
first period his work involved both purely ethnographic
studies—in other words, studies involving non-European
populations—and investigations into French folklore, from
1924 until his death he was to occupy himself exclusively
with the latter. Presumably he had become aware of the
almost total lack of researchers and work being done in
that field and as a result conceived the vast project that was
to culminate in his *Manuel*, although he did not in fact
attempt to start work on that until after he had completed a
considerable program of firsthand and indirect investigations covering large areas of the country and had successfully brought out a number of regional monographs.
His studies in the field of traditional ethnography may be
classified under three headings: first, his compilations
dealing with problems currently under debate among
ethnologists (*Tabou et totémisme à Madagascar, Mythes et
légendes d'Australie, L'Etat actuel du problème totémique*);
second, in 1909 and 1910, two much more original works,
putting forward a theory to account for certain ethnographic facts (*Les Rites de passage* and *La Formation des
légendes*); third, two books (*Etudes d'ethnographie algérienne*
and *En Algérie*) and a number of articles dealing with his
one and only field project carried out among "exotic,"
non-European populations. He spent a total of five months
among them in 1911 and 1912, and, having realized that
those two brief stays were insufficient to enable him to
"unravel all these complexities eventually discerned," he
resolved thenceforth to confine himself to the study of indigenous arts and crafts. This latter proved in the event to

be a totally isolated thread in his work, but it cleared the ground for French ethnography to lay the foundations for one of its future branches: technology.

This schematization of Van Gennep's career provides us with markers that help to establish some kind of order in the proliferation of his work, but it is also slightly reductionist in its effect. For instance, where are we to place his studies on the history of French ethnography (mostly published in *Religions, moeurs et légendes*, vol. 5), in which he introduces us to a number of eighteenth-century precursors, such as Démeunier and Lafitau? Or his article putting forward a new solution to the mystery of the Iron Mask? Or his slim volume on Homer? Or the book published in 1911 by the *Mercure de France* entitled *Les Demi-savants*, in which he pillories, quite subtly and to some comic effect, the sort of specialists in the various sciences of man who are rendered incapable of reaching the slightest understanding of the facts of their discipline by the sheer weight of their own erudition (see Appendix, "Van Gennep's Humor"). His fire in this book is directed at those scientific temperaments at the opposite extreme to his own; for although he himself possessed a vast erudition, it certainly never succeeded in stifling his intuitive understanding of folklore's facts. It would be impossible to express this more plainly than he did himself when he wrote, with reference to the plan of his bibliography for the *Manuel*, organized in accordance with the findings of personal experience: "Folklore is not an armchair science; it is an open-air and a laboratory science, in the sense that its laboratory is the whole of France itself, or one of its parts, however great or small, whether province, region, or even hamlet" (*Manuel de folklore français contemporain*, preface to vol. 3, pp. 7–8).

Let us now follow the development of his work itself, both chronologically and thematically.

TWO

TOTEMISM

During this first stage of his career, when he had not yet devoted himself exclusively to the ethnography of France, Van Gennep published a number of important articles and four books—*Tabou et totémisme à Madagascar* (1904); *Mythes et légendes d'Australie* (1906); *La Formation des légendes* (1910); and *Les Rites de passage* (1911)—the last of which forms a link between the two periods. The first three appear on first acquaintance to be simply solid dissertations on the themes of contemporary ethnology: taboos, totemism, myths and legends. Attentive reading, however, brings to light not only a number of original concepts but also great freedom of thought with regard to the accepted ideas of his day.

We must do honor where honor is due. Since totemism had been occupying the minds of ethnologists—and emptying their inkwells—for a good fifty years—from 1870, when McLennan launched the concept, until 1920, when Van Gennep published *L'Etat actuel du problème totémique*—

it is only fair that it should be given pride of place in a book devoted to someone who, simply because he belonged to that particular generation, was a spectator of the most passionate period of the totemic debate. He also took part in it, as we shall see, but his general attitude toward it was nevertheless not so much that of a participant as of a minutes-keeper, noting its broad stages, periodically recording the new theories that arose, and relating them to the more or less discordant whole already in existence. He was also an exacting critic. Indeed, his intellectual courage was such that he even dared to question Durkheim, whose authority over the whole of French sociology seemed virtually unchallengeable at that time.

Van Gennep did, however, prove a poor prophet in his preface to *L'Etat actuel du problème totémique* when he wrote that "the descriptive list of theories drawn up in the last chapter shows that totemism has exercised the sagacity and ingenuity of many scientists; and there is reason to believe that it will continue to do so for many years to come." Taking up this comment in his *Le Totémisme aujourd'hui*, Claude Lévi-Strauss remarks that "far from representing the first stage of a synthesis destined to continue, it was rather the swan song of speculation about totemism."[1] It is likely, however, that at the time Van Gennep's book appeared—in 1920, although it had been previously serialized in the *Revue de l'histoire des religions*, beginning in 1917—all ethnologists would have underwritten his assertion, so difficult is it to detect the emergence of a new current of thought by its heralding signs, which may surround us on every side yet still elude·our awareness.

It was probably the 1914–18 war that delivered the fatal blow to theoretical preoccupations with totemism. Leaving aside the more general reasons for this, such as the explosive expansion of intellectual horizons that occurred at that

time, there are other and more specific ones, in particular
the increasing number of field expeditions then being carried out under the influence of Malinowski. Not that such
expeditions had not been undertaken before, but they had
certainly been relatively rare, and all had become the object
of passionate arguments and a succession of interpretations and reinterpretations by the armchair scientists. Of
course there was a fair amount of such fieldwork going on
in America, but, generally speaking, that had remained
very little known in France, despite the zeal displayed by
Van Gennep, always an insatiable reader, in publicizing its
results. At all events, when their contact with the realities
of the field became closer and more continuous, French
ethnologists perceived that the terms of the totemic problem had been badly posed.

Van Gennep probably had a confused awareness of this,
since his most constant concern in his writings about
totemism was to formulate definitions stripped of all ambiguity, to bring the various theories into confrontation—
as we said earlier—and to lay down a basic framework. He
sensed that he was dealing with one of the major stum-
bling blocks bedeviling ethnology at that time yet was not
quite able to discern the part played in it by intellectual
fashion, even though he did admit that possibility: "That
there are 'fashions' in sciences, or, if you prefer, collective
trends, is obvious.... Yet this cannot be used as an argument against 'totemic theory,' or against the 'comparative
method,' since it would be just as easy to turn such an
argument against the unshakable partisans of the historical
method" (*Religion, moeurs et légendes*, 2:29–30).

In his review of a book dealing with the cult of military
insignia in Rome (ibid., pp. 9–12), his rejection of the
author's view that such insignia constitute a case of
totemism is made on the grounds that no "kinship of a

gens with an animal species" is ever apparent. The primary element, in short, is the belief in a kinship bond between a totem group and a human group. In 1904 Van Gennep published his report for the Religious Studies department of the Ecole pratique des hautes études, entitled *Tabou et totémisme à Madagascar*. He first lists an enormous number of taboos found to be operative in a variety of areas and then goes on to inquire, with a view to establishing the presence or absence of totemism, which of them involve animals and vegetables. His conclusion is a negative one, and for the following reasons: there is no term in Madagascar to denote the animal or vegetable taboo (or totem); the human group does not generally bear the name of the taboo animal or plant; the taboo animals or plants are not protectors of the family or clan that is bound to respect them; endogamy is much more widespread than exogamy. This means that the animal taboo occurs only as an isolated belief, *and this does not constitute totemism*. One may speak of "zoolatry with an economic bearing," of "theriolatry," of a "belief in the reincarnation of the vital form," according to the individual case, but not of totemism.

In an article of 1908 called "Tabou, totémisme, et méthode comparative" (*Religions, moeurs et légendes*, 2:22–88) Van Gennep lists the fundamental and necessary conditions for the existence of totemism within a social group and terms them the *principles* of totemism: (1) totemism is characterized by belief in a kinship bond assumed to link a group of socially and physically related humans, on the one hand, to an animal or vegetable species, or class of things, on the other; (2) this belief is expressed (*a*) in religious life by positive rites (aggregation ceremonies of the anthropo-animal, anthropo-vegetable group) and also by negative rites (prohibitions) and (*b*) in the social sphere by

fixed matrimonial rules (limited exogamy); and (3) the
totemic group bears the name of its totem.

Despite the confident tone in which these principles are
laid down, Van Gennep's writings on the question are shot
through on occasion with internal contradictions that may
indicate a certain unadmitted skepticism. In 1904, for
instance, he states: "There is not just *a* totemism but rather
a number of totemisms" (ibid., 2:13; Van Gennep's italics).
But it is in *L'Etat actuel du problème totémique* that these
contradictions are most clearly discernible, because there
they are presented in the form of criticisms directed at the
theories of his colleagues.

In his examination of Frazer's third and final theory—
termed "conceptionist" and based essentially on beliefs
among Australian aborigines, particularly the Aruntas of
Aranda, about conception and reincarnation—he quotes
the objection of an author called Heape, a specialist in
questions of animal and human reproduction, and notes
that Heape rules out as impossible the idea that men have
ever been ignorant, at any stage of civilization whatever, of
the connection between coitus and parturition, since even
the lower animals are aware of it by instinct, as is shown by
the precautions they take to protect their gestating off-
spring against future dangers. Moreover, the Australian
aborigines have developed a social and religious organization far too complex for them to be regarded as backward.
Van Gennep then goes on to quote this passage from
Heape, which has an extremely modern ring:

> Instead of supposing, with Frazer, that the ignorance
> actually claimed by these savages is proof of a real igno-
> rance of the truth, I regard it as much more probable
> that their customs, their beliefs, their ethical system if
> you will, oblige them to deny that knowledge; that a
> higher belief has been created in this way that it would

be impious for them to discuss; for that would mean
casting doubt upon the Spirits, who are more powerful
than humans. It is their belief in the omnipotence of
the spirits of the dead, or of their ancestors, living in a
particular swamp, in a rock, a cave, a stone, an animal,
or a plant, that has conditioned this belief upon which
Frazer constructs his interpretation of primitive
totemism (quoted in *L'Etat actuel du problème totémique*,
pp. 22–23).

Unfortunately, Van Gennep does not then go on to draw
out the logical consequences of this theory, so remarkable
for its time, because to have done so would have created a
domino effect and destroyed the totemic edifice totally,
piece by piece. He contents himself with using it as an
argument against Frazer (and also against Durkheim): "If
the Arunta have systematized their belief in fertilization
without the intervention of the male to this extent, and
have made it such an important element in their magico-
religious ceremonies, it is because the Arunta are more
developed and less primitive than the other aborigines"
(*L'Etat actuel*, p. 24).

Van Gennep, as I mentioned earlier, was never cir-
cumspect in his criticisms of Durkheim. He begins by at-
tacking him on this very point: so-called primitive societies
are not simple societies; they are just as complex as
"civilized" societies from the point of view of their internal
mechanism and the interweaving of their functions; they
are neither uniform nor homogeneous. Van Gennep then
follows up this statement with a broad hypothesis on the
way societies evolve, a hypothesis not unlike modern
theories on the origins of man, but one he was never to
develop further or seek to confirm:

Man has invented a great number of institutions,
many of which have followed their particular line of

development until they reached a dead end, and only
a few of which have proved capable of surviving in
order to constitute what is correctly termed civilization.
Among the institutions that have led to such dead ends
we find exogamy and totemism, along with the caste
system and polyandry. Attempting to base a general
theory of religion and society upon such phenomena,
as Durkheim did, could only lead to an erroneous view
of reality, to a strained interpretation of the facts (ibid.,
p. 43).

The very foundation of Durkheim's book *Les formes élémentaires de la vie religieuse* is therefore unsound, since although
the aborigines are, from the technical point of view, primitive in the literal sense of that word, they are far from being
so as far as their matrimonial rules, the organization of
their totemism, and their ceremonial life are concerned. It
is therefore impossible to find the seeds of religion in their
practices.

Van Gennep is equally critical when it comes to the actual content of Durkheim's totemism. As we know, the
great sociologist saw the totem as originating in an emblem
that the social group assigned to itself in order to ensure its
existence, its cohesion, and its survival, an emblem in
which it recognized the representation of an animal which,
as a result of this identification, became endowed with the
sacred character of the emblem. This account of how totemism developed is identical with that put forward by
Lang, except that in the latter's theory it is the name of an
animal that the group usually assigns to itself, thus automatically making that animal an object of veneration. To
the all-important question "Why was this emblem taken
from the animal or vegetable kingdom, but more specifically from the former?" Durkheim replies, according to
Van Gennep, with the "merest commonplaces of ethno-

graphical literature," "a string of dogmatic formulas constructed without regard to the facts and with nothing more
than a very weak probability in their favor." Durkheim
thought in fact that the chosen animal is one that plays an
essential economic role in the life of these hunters and
fishermen; that there is a greater natural kinship between
man and animal than between man and plant; and that
each group probably selected as its emblem the animal
most widespread in its particular locality (economic theory,
psychological and biological theory, and localist theory).

The disagreement between Van Gennep and Durkheim
was apparently total. We have already seen that the former
had always remained outside the sociological school that
exercised so extensive a domination over all French work
in this field. In the present case we are dealing with a
genuine incompatibility, which springs, to my way of
thinking, from Van Gennep's extraordinary intuition
where ethnographical reality was concerned. And it must
genuinely have been intuition, since he never undertook
any "exotic" fieldwork himself, if we ignore the two short
trips to Algeria; and yet he possessed the mysterious ability, when faced with any theory, to discern immediately
those elements in it that were purely speculative and un-
supported by ethnographic facts. It was this enigmatic faculty that placed him closer to the British anthropological
school, even though he often criticized its individual repre-
sentatives. It was he who in 1898 translated Frazer's first
major work on totemism. And not only did he read all the
British and American ethnological works that appeared, he
frequently reviewed them for French publications. He recognized the members of the British school as being more
attached to ethnographical reality than their French coun-
terparts, partly because more of them undertook fieldwork, and partly no doubt as a result of the traditional

British leaning toward empiricism. In the second half of
L'Etat actual du problème totémique he sweeps aside in one
sentence the hollow constructions not only of Durkheim
but also of innumerable other writers who had successively
addressed themselves to solving this problem:

> It is quite clear that totemism is not a simple phenom-
> enon but on the contrary an extremely complex one, a
> phenomenon that varies from country to country and
> people to people, precisely because it is a product of
> human ingenuity; to explain it with verbal formulas
> such as *collective thought, totemic mode of thought, sociali-
> zation of affective values*, is to retrogress to the days of
> phlogiston, if not to those of the *virtus dormitiva*
> (p. 317).

He nevertheless displays great patience in his thorough
presentation of all these successive theories, not forgetting
that of "Monsieur Sigismond Freud," the inventor of
psychoanalysis, or the then more recent ones of Kroeber
and Boas, in which one can already perceive signs that the
very data of the problem were on the verge of dissolution.
In this second section he also examines the possible vestiges of totemism that some workers were stubbornly
striving to reveal in the social and religious institutions of
ancient Egypt and Greece.

It is only at the very end of his book that Van Gennep
offers his own ideas on the subject. They do not really add
up to a theory, however, in the sense that there is no hint
of the systematic or the doctrinaire in the views he expresses. If we set these ideas beside those he put forward
in 1908 (see pp. 25–26, above), we observe not a radical
change but rather a broadening of his views on the question, a wider comprehension of the facts, using the word
comprehension in both its senses: understanding and in-
clusion.

The function of totemism, in Van Gennep's view, is to maintain the cohesion of the social group as it stands and to guarantee its continuity. The idea of totemic kinship satisfied the social need for human classification.

> For every ordered society has an absolute necessity to classify not only its human members but also the things and beings of the natural world . . .; nothing permits us to regard any given system of classification, for example the zoological system of totemism, the cosmographic system, or the professional system (castes), as anterior to the others. This classification sets up a specific bond between all the individuals situated under the same heading, a bond that is closely related in its psychological essence to the kinship bond (p. 346).

The notion of totemic kinship is a compound of physiological kinship (the least precise), social kinship (by initiation, adoption, marriage, and so on), and cosmic kinship (or kinship by classification), "which links all the men of a particular group to all the creatures or things situated within that group theoretically." But there is no question of these three elements having been simply added together. Rather, they are combined in the same way that copper, sulfur, and oxygen are combined to form copper sulfate. Since another factor in social cohesion is the possession of a given territory, there exist not only various modes of totemic appropriation but also other systems of appropriation that have nothing to do with totemism at all. In other words, Van Gennep is harking back momentarily to Frazer's conceptionist theory: it is because the social group has appropriated a territory to itself that it then overlays that territory with a "map" of the haunts of "child-spirits," and not the reverse. "Even a poor and largely uncultivated territory is valued by its human occupants at any given moment less as a present home than as an eternal home for all the generations to come" (p. 348). As far as Australia is concerned, the myths describing the journeyings of totemic ancestors are myths of appropriation applying to a particular territory. The purpose of the related ceremonies is the maintenance of the fauna, the flora, and the particular topographical features of that territory.

Van Gennep then goes on to deal with the role of names and emblems, which cannot be a cause of totemism, as Durkheim claimed, but only a consequence, "not merely of totemism but of any form of collective organization" (p. 349) whose function is to serve as a symbolic bond.

If social cohesion requires so many elements to ensure its maintenance, this is because it has to wage constant battle against the tendency to dissolution and fragmentation. Social classification strengthens a group's internal cohesiveness but at the same time weakens its bonds with all other groups. Totemism makes it possible to maintain "the relation not only of the component parts of society with the social whole, but also of that social whole with the whole of nature" (p. 350).

Exogamy plays an identical role as far as the human members of the totemic group are concerned. It has a positive aspect, as Van Gennep clearly discerns, that earlier authors ignored because they conceived of it as being essentially a prohibition. The function of exogamy is to institute a relation between social groups "that would otherwise have no more chance of coming into contact than the stonemasons of Rouen with the hairdressers of Marseilles," as he expressed it in a lively image, later taken up and systematically explored by Lévi-Strauss in *Les Structures élémentaires de la parenté* and *Le Totémisme aujourd'hui* (pp. 49–50). This notion leads on to a very simple explanation of the fact that exogamy is sometimes associated with "totemic" institutions and sometimes not.

Thus if we find exogamy coinciding with totemism in a tribe, it is because that tribe has decided to strengthen the social cohesion already achieved through totemism by supplementing it with a further system, one that is linked to the first by the factor of physical and social kinship while being distinguished from it, though not opposed to it, by the elimination of cosmic (or classificatory) kinship (p. 351).

The same is true of the other institutions that various theoreticians, with varying degrees of success, had annexed to the sytems they had constructed: secret societies, magical brotherhoods, agrarian ceremonies, classificatory system, uterine filiation. And Van Gennep concludes:

In short, totemism is a clearly distinct, perfectly viable, and specific mode of combining collective kinship and territoriality, instituted and perfected with the aim of resolving the fundamental problem of all general societies (tribe, city, nation): how to ensure social cohesion and survival despite the replacement of individuals, the tendency of secondary groups (family, clan, caste, and so on) to seek autonomy, crises of the internal environment, and hostility of the external environment (p. 352).

Thus Van Gennep was able to rid himself without difficulty of the historical problem in which his predecessors and contemporaries had become so thoroughly bogged down, obliged as they were by their various theories to puzzle their brains over the origins of totemism, the first forms of religion, and the degree of primitiveness of the Aranda and aborigine societies generally. It was Van Gennep's view, in fact, that all the elements of any social system have a meaning, since they all help to strengthen the social cohesion of the group as a whole or of its subgroups. He does not thereby deny that there are occasional inventions or borrowings—though these prove viable only insofar as they can be integrated into the system—or degenerations or deviations, but social regulation will succeed in eliminating those, too. What counts for Van Gennep is the society seen synchronically and as a dynamically functioning entity. What interest him are the mechanisms that enable the society to survive and develop. Unfortunately, however, he was unable to express all this explicitly, since that would have meant abandoning totemism altogether as a useless concept and replacing it with that of the social mechanism.[2] He stops at that precise point, halted in his tracks by a failure of nerve for which it is hard to blame him when we consider the importance assigned to the totemic problem by all sociological and ethnological research during the previous fifty years or so. In a note on page 346 he even states explicitly that he regards the retention of the term totemism and of the notion it denotes in ethnographic and hierological terminology as justified—a confession that he had been tempted to dispense with it.

In his *La Pensée sauvage* Lévi-Strauss remarks (p. 215) that Van Gennep "remained a prisoner of the traditional categories of thought within the framework of which he dutifully inserted his proof." In fact, Van Gennep perceived not only totemism's function as a force for social cohesion but also its classifying function. He went even further, since he opposed Durkheim in making classification not a consequence but a "primary and essential constituent element":

> For peoples without totemism also possess their particular system of classification, which is likewise one of the primary elements of their system of general social organization and reacts in that role on their magico-religious and lay institutions. There are the systems

found in the East; for example, Chinese and Persian dualism, Assyro-Babylonian cosmographism, the so-called magical system of sympathetic correspondences, and so on (p. 345, n. 1).

Here again, however, he proves timorous and once more lacks the courage to rid himself of that cumbersome theoretical machine and its fruitless churnings. Yet this idea was one that he had been stating as early as 1908: "[Totemism], moreover, implies a specific intellectual orientation expressed in its own logical categories and a specific system of cosmological classification" (*Revue de l'histoire des religions* 58 [1908]: 34–76; reprinted in *Religions, moeurs et légendes*, 2:22–88). We are very close here to Lévi-Strauss's totemic operator and yet very far away too: there remains only one more bridge to be crossed, but it is apparently an impassable one.

THREE

COMPARATIVE METHOD, SEQUENCE METHOD, MYTHS AND RITES

Totemism was not the only problem requiring Van Gennep's attention. In fact, thanks to his constantly questing curiosity, even the most apparently mundane events could set that brain of his whirring. Ethnography for him was not some form of abstract inquiry but a way of life. "The greatest charm of ethnography," he wrote,

> is perhaps that once its simplest rudiments have been acquired and its specific method grasped, one's daily life takes on a new aspect. Some trifling isolated fact, or some chance remark overheard in passing, because one perceives its links with an entire network of beliefs and customs, can conjure up a whole world of analogies and memories" (*Religions, moeurs et légendes*, 2:239).

The everyday loses its opacity, is illuminated and revealed as organized. It is the five volumes of *Religions, moeurs et légendes* (1908–14), in which Van Gennep gathered together what he considered to be his most interesting articles to date, that best display this omnivorous curiosity at work. For example, apropos the election of Pope Pius X, who at first declined the honor that had befallen him, Van Gennep refuses to view this as a purely individual action. He recounts other examples of such ritual refusal and interprets it as a ritual aimed at the socialization of responsibility.

However, these volumes also include more-theoretical articles, and it is here, particularly, that we must look for an account of the methodology advocated by Van Gennep in the ethnological field. This is in fact the comparative method, a product of the British anthropological school much more than of French sociology. Van Gennep defines it by contrasting it with the historical method. The latter looks at phenomena in their chronological order and makes use of written or representational evidence. The comparative method disregards temporal and local conditions and makes use of oral evidence in addition. "The historical method juxtaposes, the ethnographic method compares. The former concerns itself with *forms*, the latter with *functions* and *mechanisms*" (ibid., 2:82).

The ethnographic method takes its models from biology, since, like biology, it is studying *living* phenomena. But just as biology needs to make use of historical sciences, such as geology and paleontology, in order to classify living things, so anthropology too needs the historical method. It is true to say that if we wish to study a given social institution in isolation from all other institutions, then we must make use of the historical method in order to describe the stages through which it has passed. But what we are then left with is nothing more than a description. If we wish to obtain an explanation, then we need to make a comparison with the development of that institution in other populations or civilizations in order to determine

which are external and local elements and which are intrinsic. "Thus, when we wish to study social phenomena, we
must study them both locally, with the help of the historical method, and also comparatively, with the aid of the
biological method, so that we can classify them into
'natural' categories: family, genus, species" (ibid., pp.
84–85).

For Van Gennep, the great merit of the precursors of
French ethnology lay precisely in the fact that they applied
the comparative method. Montesquieu, when seeking to
establish the origins and workings of social institutions,
consulted the reports of travelers. In this he was imitating
Lafitau, who compared biblical and classical evidence with
his own firsthand observations of the North American In-
dians. This interest of French scholars in the comparative
study of peoples was brought to a halt by Auguste Comte.
During the greater part of the nineteenth century his
theory of mankind's stages of development deflected
research away from a direct study of societies, and it was
only recently that the comparative method had been re-
vived in France, under the influence of the British anthropological school. In the last volume of *Religions, moeurs
et légendes* Van Gennep was to devote a long study to these
French precursors of ethnography, the most interesting of
whom is probably Démeunier, who wrote: "After so many
books on man, we have not yet begun to compare the
morals, the manners, the customs, and the laws of the
different peoples: I intend to repair this omission."

However, Van Gennep did not accept the method of the
British anthropological school unreservedly. He makes this
clear in his review of Frazer's *Golden Bough* (ibid., 5:43).
The method employed by Frazer consists in taking a given
theme, breaking it down into its elements, analyzing each
of those elements, then seeking to establish a succession of

parallels to them. The work as a whole comes to resemble a
genealogical tree with an inordinate number of branches.
And the question arises as to what value the demonstra-
tion of such parallels possesses. The French sociological
school (Durkheim and his followers) denounced "these
wild peregrinations from people to people, these aimless
excursions, these vast compilations." The criticism is
analogous to that directed by these same contributors to
the *Année sociologique* against Van Gennep's *Les Rites de
passage*, and it therefore seems likely that it is less Frazer's
method than his own that Van Gennep is justifying in his
review. The first step, he wrote, consists in studying the
fact or group of facts under consideration in a particular
locality "in order to indicate the relations between this fact
and anterior facts" (ibid., 5:32). Having studied further
facts, again with the aid of this same historico-cultural
method, and classified them into series, one then
proceeds, step by step, to establish the existence of cycles.
The second stage of the procedure consists in isolating
those elements that are independent of time and place and
common to all the facts studied. Van Gennep compares
this procedure to that employed in mineralogy, which
likewise begins by establishing local factors but then employs "petrographic analysis, which is not concerned with
the place of discovery but studies the specimen solely with
regard to its constituents" (p. 33). It is a duty incumbent
upon all specialists in the sciences of man to raise themselves, as the natural sciences do, from the individual, the
topographically and temporally localized, to more general
ideas. Van Gennep suggests calling such ideas "schemas,"
but they are the same thing as the "concordances" of linguistics, the "parallels" of the British anthropological
school, the *"Völkergedanke"* of the German ethnologists,
and so on. "When one wishes to discover mental, social,

cultural, and literary concordances, permanences, laws, there is no other method possible than comparison, and as wide-ranging as possible" (p. 34). Such is Frazer's procedure and his aim, Van Gennep says, and, whatever criticisms may be made of him, it is incumbent upon us to recognize that merit.

At this time Van Gennep was using the terms "comparative method," "ethnographic method," and "biological method" more or less synonomously. He saw them as a means that would enable one to compare all the facts of any one order, regardless of time and space, throughout the gigantic laboratory constituted by all the myriad human groups scattered across the world's continents. It is easy to criticize the self-evident lack of theoretical foundation for this method, but Van Gennep laid no claims to having provided one. What he was seeking above all was a means of clearing a way through the dense jungle of ethnographic facts at an almost empirical level. Thus he never speaks of laws but of "schemas" (as in *Les Rites de passage*, for instance), and in an article entitled "De la méthode dans l'étude des rites et des mythes" (*Religions, moeurs et légendes*, 4:47–81) he employs the terms "tool," "key," and "convenient technical procedure." He then goes on to describe three of these "convenient technical procedures." He calls the first *the nascent-fact method*, and it is analogous to one used in the natural sciences, whose practitioners sometimes provoke a phenomenon they wish to study. Folklorists can sometimes observe the birth of an etiological legend or belief in the same way and then study the mental and social mechanism that is conditioning its origin and development. Of course it is not possible, as it is in the natural sciences, actually to provoke phenomena in order to observe them. The genesis of the fact one wishes to study must be natural, and one must study it in its environment in order to examine the circumstances that accompany and condition it. This is the *ethological method*, which does not consist merely in a return to the eighteenth- and nineteenth-century theory of determination by physical environment. For example, Spencer and Gillen had observed the close interdependence between the totemic system of the Australian aborigines and the climate, flora, and fauna of their habitat; in view of this, it is certainly desirable that we should have some knowledge of the economic importance of the totem animal. The third technical procedure Van Gennep mentions in this article is the *sequence method*, which consists in studying each theme, whether ritual or mythological, in its relation to what precedes and what follows it. One can then compare whole sequences within a single order (marriage ceremony with marriage ceremony, initiation rite with other initiation rites), thereby enabling one to establish the universal and necessary dominants. It was in his *Les Rites de passage* that Van Gennep expounded and illustrated this sequence method most fully (see chap. 4, below).

In *La Formation des légendes*, which dates from 1910, Van Gennep shows himself to be equally in favor of empirical method. This is a book teeming with ideas; but since few of them are followed through to their conclusions, it does leave one with a certain impression of confusion. The aim of the work is an ambitious one, since it is attempting to provide answers to the following questions:

> What do we mean by fable, fairy tale, legend, and myth, and to what extent are these various forms of so-called folktales interdependent? What is the place of legends in men's lives generally, and how are they linked with society's other activities? What is their value as geographical, ethnographical, historical, or psychological evidence? What are the laws governing

the genesis, formation, transmission, and modification of legends? What is the relative importance, in literary production generally, of the individual and the collective elements?

To the last two of these questions Van Gennep provides partial answers—for want of genuine solutions—that were really very original in their day.

As far as the classification of the various narratives is concerned, Van Gennep is more or less in agreement with his contemporaries in making a distinction between the folktale on the one hand (whether about animals or the supernatural) and legend and myth on the other. The distinction between folktale and legend was of a spatiotemporal nature: the legend claims to be an account of facts localized in both time and space, whereas in the folktale there are no such limitations. The myth, like the legend, occurs within a time and a space, but both dimensions are in this case beyond human range, so that the characters peopling them are gods, heroes, or beings half-human and half-animal. Another line of demarcation was usually drawn between stories that are objects of belief (legends and myths) and those that are not (folktales and fables). In addition, myths were classified as objects of belief that could be enacted as magical and religious rites. In practice, however, according to Van Gennep, these distinctions are not always operative. He therefore adopts an approximate definition, leaving himself free to narrow it down later, when and if the need should arise: "I shall take *legend* to mean a localized, individualized narrative that is also an object of belief, and *myth* to mean a legend that bears a relation to the supernatural and is expressed in action by rites" (*La Formation des légendes*, p. 30).

The great problem that specialists of folk literature (almost exclusively that of the Indo-European languages) had been debating ever since the days of the Brothers Grimm was that of the origin of folktales and their themes. As we know, the "Aryan" theory of the Grimms and Max Müller was succeeded by the "Indianist" theory, represented in France by Eugène Cosquin, and by the "anthropological" theory of Andrew Lang. The position taken by Van Gennep on this subject was an original one. He begins by reminding us that American ethnographers and folklorists (Lowie and Kroeber) employed the term "catchword" to designate the recurring themes in the various tales they collected. But these "catchwords" are in fact by no means confined to a single theme: they are really combinations of themes. Van Gennep consequently proposes the concept of the "thematic cycle," on the model of his concept of the "ceremonial sequence" put forward the previous year in *Les Rites de passage* (see chap. 4, below). However, any particular theme may in practice occur in several of these cycles, and its importance may also vary in each one. Not only that, but its meaning will change in accordance with the place it occupies in each cycle. This means that mere comparison of individual themes is wasted effort; what matters is to establish parallels between defined combinations of themes. Seen in this way, the problems of origin and diffusion present themselves in a new light. Just as it is risky to attribute a place of origin to any theme found in various regions of the globe, so, by the same token, it is difficult to contest diffusion when one encounters an identical sequence of themes. In any event, the very greatest prudence is called for in these complex matters, and theories as to places of origin and laws of formation, propagation, and combination of folklore themes are always too simple. For instance, variations in the material may relate first to typical details (Cinderella's glass slipper), second to the themes, and finally to the sequences. Thus we may find two tales having the same sequence but very different descriptive details or, on the contrary, tales in which the sequences are broken but the details have been preserved.

It is not until the last chapter of *La Formation des légendes* that Van Gennep puts forward the "laws" governing the formation of legends, employing the term "law" with regret, since he would have preferred "schema," already employed in *Les Rites de passage*, but "some other ethnographers and folklorists have not felt the same scruple." The first of these laws is that of localization and delocalization: we sometimes find that a narrative will include a theme whose action is localized (etiological legends intended as explanations of the origin of some particular topographical feature or rock formation), whereas in another tale the same theme will be totally devoid of localization. The second law is similar but applies to the protagonists of the stories: it is that of personification and depersonification. Thus in certain Greek folktales we find themes associated with Odysseus but with the characters unnamed: Polyphemus is an anonymous demon, Odysseus just a very resourceful and adventurous young man. The law of temporalization and detemporalization applies to the presence or absence of spatiotemporal indications in the narratives. We have already seen that legends, as opposed to folktales, will include these. But this does not mean that they possess any strict historical value. For example, they will sometimes portray facts separated in time as coeval and at other times will separate facts that were historically contemporaneous: "There is therefore...sometimes a shrinkage, sometimes a dilation of the temporal element" (p. 162). At this time Van Gennep was of the opinion that though legends (and myths) distort historical truth, they can nevertheless be taken to bear witness to it. His thought on this subject had already undergone a shift since his *Mythes et légendes d'Australie*; there he saw no reason to refuse historical value to aborigines' tales and thought it possible in this way to reconstruct their tribal migrations, for example, or the earlier states of their institutions. In *L'Etat actual du problème totémique*, on the other hand, he violently rejects this idea, having been convinced by Strehlow's evidence that "myths and legends—those of the aborigines at least—have no more scientific or evidential value from the social point of view than from the ethnic, zoological, or botanical point of view" (p. 140). During the latter part of his career, devoted exclusively to French ethnography, Van Gennep became increasingly chary of history, as we shall see, though without ever successfully "eliminating the problem."

The last of the laws he proposes is that of the convergence and dissociation of themes. It is also the most interesting. Let us suppose a series O of thematic motifs a, b, c, d, and e. If this series moves away from its original environment, each of the motifs may be lost, so that the series will vanish as an organic grouping, while the individual motifs become integrated into other series, which we may designate X, Y, and Z. All Van Gennep's laws may act separately or together.

> Thus, in the series O: the nonlocalized theme a becomes localized as it is incorporated into X; b, originally nonindividualized, becomes individualized; c, originally nontemporalized, becomes temporalized, and all three converge in X with the analogous themes a', b', c', whereas d fails to become integrated into X, and c' converges with its analogue c to produce a new series O, which then includes a, c. . . . The number of combinations is thus, a priori, infinite (*La Formation des légendes*, pp. 280–81).

One has the feeling that Van Gennep has grasped the formal mechanism of these transformations perfectly but

that, when he attempts to establish their causes, he side-
tracks himself into vague psychological explanations. He
explains that since all peoples have their own particular
tendencies toward gaiety or melancholy, brutality or ten-
derness, a diffuse or trenchant style, each will select from
the themes it encounters those that best suit it. Consequently, folktales collected in the extreme north of
Russia, where conditions are very harsh, are all grim and
austere in flavor. This clearly shows that Van Gennep had
totally failed to grasp the consequences and import of these
laws of transformation (rather than formation). This is
verified a little later on, when he examines the law governing the reversal of themes put forward by Leo Frobenius.
Van Gennep will accept this law as applicable solely to
secondary episodes, and he quotes the example of the
motif—found by Cosquin in India— of the "shoes that
must be worn out." A women, searching for her husband,
will never find him until she has worn out a pair of iron
shoes (or seven pairs, in some variants). But among the
Kalmyks (a Mongol tribe) the theme has been reversed
and, in the process, has become attached to another character: it is the husband who arrives carrying on his back a
bundle of boots worn out in the service of the gods and
heroes. For Van Gennep, the cases involved are so rare
that the principle of reversal does not merit the name of
law.

We must nevertheless allow him the great merit of having stated and attempted to prove that folk literature does
not undergo random transformations dictated purely by
chance and that there are formal laws governing the
phenomena of borrowing and diffusion: "in this domain,
as in others, the forms encountered, however varied and
diverse, combine in accordance with a very small number
of mechanisms and are governed by a very small number
of general rules, or *laws*" (p. 310).

He also pointed out the following paradox: that oral literature varies a great deal, whereas folk tradition in general displays a tendency toward stability. Van Gennep's
explanation of this paradox was based on an idea quite
new at that time. Folk literature, he tells us, is in fact called
that only by virtue of the folk or popular environment in
which it exists and evolves. Environment apart, however,
the contribution of the individual is almost as important as
in written literature, the important difference being that
the form of folk literature is wholly oral. It follows that the
study of folktales should in future include a study of their
social function, because that function has a meaning. Let
us imagine a tale of a certain form and content. If it is told
anywhere, at any time of day, on no particular occasion,
then it is just a folktale. If, on the other hand, it is told at
some solemn moment and is accompanied by a ritual celebrated by characters regarded as sacred, then it is a myth.
"The form of the story is the same in both cases, with all its
details remaining identical; but the function, that is to say
the social role, is different" (p. 307).

It is striking how early Van Gennep took up a position as
firm as it was original on the problem of the individual and
collective elements in folk creations. In an article of 1910, in
which he gives an account of certain legends, songs, and
games collected in Haute-Savoie (*Religions, moeurs et
légendes*, 3:181–263) he recalls that in *La Formation des
légendes* he had protested against the common error of
equating the terms "folk" and "collective." "It is an error
to believe that a collectivity invents or creates: every time
one pursues one's analysis far enough, one finds that the
source of inventions and modifications of every kind is an
individual or a very few individuals . . .; 'folk' (or 'popular')
means only that which is current among the folk (or
people)" (p. 242). He then reiterates this conviction with
reference to the songs he has collected in Savoy: as with

folktales, oral transmission of songs is accompanied by dis-
tortions, which do not occur randomly but in directions
and in accordance with trends that are determined by as-
certainable factors. In the case of songs one should attempt
to seek out the underlying psychological and phonetic
rules.

In dissociating the collective from the popular or folk in
this way, Van Gennep was attempting to destroy an old
myth that has died hard, since one can still find traces of it
even today. One can only admire his independence of
thought in relation to the accepted scientific ideas of his
day and wonder as to the origin of this conviction, which
seems to have sprung into his work already fully formed. It
is there as early as 1906, in *Mythes et légendes d'Australie*,
where he asserts that the role of the individual in primitive
societies is not as slight as is generally believed. Among the
aborigines an intelligent individual is able to suggest
modifications in a ceremonial that are then adopted by the
collectivity. And to this action on the part of individuals we
must add the interactions occurring within any large
group. In frontier zones, "in both the geographical and
sociological senses of that term" (cf. the importance of the
frontier zone in transition rituals, p. 65, below), the various
customs or institutions undergo a process of adaptation as
a result of continuing contact and are then assimilated by
the separate groups concerned. Social modifications are
thus the result of two factors: individual invention and
collective assimilation.

In a 1908 article entitled "De quelques cas de bovaryisme
collective" (*Religions, moeurs et légendes*, 1:202–29) Van
Gennep broadens the data of the problem to include all
human transformations. "We find beliefs, customs, institutions, spreading, meeting, combining, forming structures,
neutralizing one another, kept in motion by an incessant

agitation whose underlying cause at first seems incomprehensible, so that one is tempted to think it the result of chance alone" (p. 209). He then expresses a hope that Jules de Gaultier's theory of "collective bovaryism" will help us to establish the laws underlying these transformations, or at least to isolate their dominants. Since de Gaultier's theory has now fallen into near oblivion, it may perhaps be helpful to recall it here. Bovaryism is "the power allotted to man to conceive himself as other than he is"; it may be either individual or collective (and the term itself is derived, needless to say, from the name of Flaubert's heroine, Emma Bovary). Collective bovaryism exists when a certain number of individuals within a group fall under the spell of some foreign custom. From that moment the collectivity is divided within itself, and the result is a decrease in collective productivity, misdirected and fruitless effort, and sometimes complete disintegration. This is in fact precisely what Van Gennep observed when studying Liberia, which recent reports had shown to be in an advanced state of economic and cultural decline. The reason, he said, was that the country was being torn apart by the conflict between its bovaryistic conception (imitation of the white life-style) and its true psyche. The ideal image toward which the Liberians were striving was that of the puritan Anglo-Saxons; their social debility was caused by their wish to be other than they were. In Van Gennep's eyes it is always possible to borrow the external elements of another civilization (methods of transport, say) but not what we would call its ideology. This theory led him to a violent denunciation of European colonialism:

By forcing the Blacks of the tropical countries, or the Oceanians, to adopt our conception of modesty and thus to clothe themselves, we kill them. That is a

particularly brutal case, in that the indigenous physiol-
ogy and psychology are mortally affected at one blow.
But usually our psychic influence is not expressed in one
isolated and easily observable action. It is ordinarily
only little by little that the indigenous actions and ways
of feeling are modified, that individual and collective
antagonisms are exacerbated, that the groups disinte-
grate and die. It is only slowly that a new conception of
the world, destructive of the local conception, gradually
infiltrates them (p. 227).

A better description of the process of ethnocide would be
hard to find.

Later, apropos a letter from Edouard Meyer on the origins of the state (*Religions, moeurs et légendes*, 1:230–98), he
returned to this problem of the representations that individuals form of the social, linguistic, or national grouping to which they belong. What they are conscious of is
unity and identity when reality in fact discloses cross-
breeding, borrowing, mixture. There must therefore exist
in the social mechanism both a tendency toward differentiation and a tendency toward uniformity, both of
which are necessary to the society's survival. Yet again one
senses Van Gennep's curiosity spurring him on to analyze
social processes at all their various levels and to seek out
the rules, the "schemas," the laws, that govern them.

Among the questions that held the attention of Van
Gennep's contemporaries, that of the relations between
myth and ritual was by no means the least debated, even
though it is true to say that it captured the interest of
British and German ethnologists rather more than that of
their colleagues in France. The point of view adopted by
Hubert and Mauss was a strictly sociological one; the distinction they made was between narratives that are objects
of belief, the myth and the legend, and those that are sim-

ply esthetic productions, the tale and the epic. They state that any regularly celebrated rite is accompanied with great frequency by a myth but that the question of which antedates the other must not be posed abstractly and cannot be answered in any general way. Sometimes the myth is no longer a direct representation of the ritual; certain rituals are accompanied by myths of varying age, while independent myths can create rituals "by analogy." With reference to this last point, Van Gennep poses the following question: if the myth alone persists and does not produce the birth of a fresh ritual, what does it become? What are we to call it, since only myths that have corresponding rituals—that are, in other words, religious in function—can merit the name of myth?

Van Gennep's first study devoted to this question is to be found in *Les Mythes et légendes d'Australie* (introduction, pp. XCI–CXVI). Rather than launch into a theoretical argument, however, he prefers to concentrate on the concrete facts of aboriginal myths and rituals, the relations of which he establishes by means of a genuinely dialectic method.

He observes first of all that in Australia, particularly among the central tribes, the myth presents itself "strictly as a narrated ritual, and the ritual as an enacted myth." Now, Spencer and Gillen had pointed out that "gifted" individuals may invent rituals, or fragments of ritual, to be inserted into already existing ceremonies, the mechanism of this invention being either conscious—albeit bounded by the individual's sociocultural context—or oneiric. When this happens, Van Gennep says, the ritual is anterior to the myth: "First the individual ceremonial action, a modification of the customary action, then the explanatory narrative, the myth" (p. XCV). Moreover, it can sometimes happen that no narrative is created to correspond to the added ceremony. On the other hand, it seems that no myth

is ever recited without reference to the ritual; among the
Aranda, and above all the Dieri, myths are oral rituals. He
concludes from this that it is impossible to establish any
anteriority of the one to the other: "That would amount to
asking whether speech is anterior to thought or vice versa.
Such questions are themes for academic discussion and
nothing more" (p. c).

In *La Formation des légendes* he extends the data of the
problem and goes into the question of the origins of the
theater. He assigns the name "myth" to "dramatized
legends," which is to say narratives that are objects of belief and also expressed in ritual action. In Mexican
ceremonies, for example, one finds a combination of spoken and sung narrative, incantations, dance, and theatrical
presentation, in which the congregation participates.
These elements then became dissociated in accordance
with a variety of set ways. In Greek drama the rituals
evolved into mimed representations. The Christian mystery plays, on the other hand, preserved their value as acts
of piety through almost the entire Middle Ages. In Protes-
tant services, recitation of the sacred texts is not "acted
out," while Roman Catholic ceremonies, on the other
hand, have largely preserved this link between narrative
and ritual. Finally, the theater as we know it dispensed
almost entirely with acting out recited narrative.

Having briefly sketched this "schema" or outline plan of
the evolution of the "dramatized legend," Van Gennep
then moves on to the question of whether the myth is
anterior to the ritual or vice versa and revises the position
he had taken up in *Mythes et légendes d'Australie*, where he
had dismissed it as futile—wrongly, he now sees, since
simple common sense makes it obvious that any ritual
requires a previously established scenario. It can happen
among the aborigines that certain individuals will suggest

to their collectivity—through the intermediary of religious chiefs, magicians, and so on—ceremonial modifications or original fragments of ritual. This process clearly involves the use of speech, and "thus the narrative is necessarily anterior to the action" (*La Formation des légendes*, p. 117). Presumably Van Gennep uses the terms "narrative" and "action" here, rather than "myth" and "ritual," out of a possible fear of protest against this implicit definition *a minima*. It is a definition that certainly strikes one by its amazing modernity. It presupposes, in effect, that a myth has an existence in the unconscious of an individual as participant in a sociocultural context. It is specifically among the Aranda that "gifted" individuals—either in a dream or simply thanks to a conscious inventive process—receive from certain Spirits dating from "the time of dreams" (cf. Roheim) the idea and scenario for a new ceremony.

Van Gennep then remarks on the contrast between what he calls primitive "magico-religious dramas" and the theater as we know it. In the former, the actions are ritual in character and never change, whereas the narrative undergoes modification; in the latter, on the contrary, it is the text that never changes, since it has been fixed in print, whereas the physical action does vary (interpretation of roles, staging). Here is how he explains the origin of myth variants: they arise from interpretations, over a period of time or in a variety of places, of ritual representations that have ceased to be understood; or, in other cases, the rituals themselves remain intact, but a more recent ideology—Christianity, for example—imposes a new mythic interpretation upon them.

Although sometimes encumbered by certain notions current in his day but now obsolete, Van Gennep's analyses of what he in fact never actually called mythology are striking in their subtlety. Indeed, we have good reason to regret that he later abandoned this area of ethnology and devoted his attention increasingly—as we shall see—to "practices" or "observances" rather than to oral literature.

That Van Gennep possessed—quite spontaneously and intuitively it would seem—a both rigorous and authentic view of ethnography as a discipline, as well as of ethnographic reality, is made very clear in a 1913 article called "Quelques lacunes de l'ethnographie actuelle" (*Religions, moeurs et légendes*, vol. 5). At that time he was teaching at the University of Neuchâtel, while also concerning himself with the reorganization of the ethnographic museum there, and the article reflects the preoccupations then uppermost in his mind: the dearth of both instructors and students in the ethnographic field and the problems facing the museographer. Above all, he is concerned with denouncing two disastrous trends apparent in ethnography at that time: the historical trend and the museological trend.

The first, he complains, tries to explain the present by means of the past, whereas ethnography examines "a given fact in its own present reality and establishes all the factors actually in operation at the moment of observation—all of them, without exception: material and psychical, individual and collective, conscious and semiconscious" (p. 18). His position has not changed on this point, since in an article written in 1908, "Tabou, totémisme et méthode comparative" (*Religions, moeurs et légendes*, 2:86), he was already saying that explanation means "establishing the forces that have acted in one direction or the other." But this was a by no means comfortable attitude, since it involved a total reversal of the traditional values taught by those educational systems that regarded the present as a function of the past and employed principles of classification inappropriate to the aims of ethnography. In the intervening years Van Gennep had thus moved even further away from history. In the 1908 article he was merely seeing it as an inappropriate method of providing explanations for ethnographic facts. Now he was regarding it as downright dangerous, because its procedure is the very reverse of the ethnographer's.

The second danger he saw threatening the discipline was the museological trend. It was encouraging students to direct their interest exclusively onto objects, and, more particularly, rare and ancient objects, collector's items. The responsibility for this, he believed, must be laid at the door of the ethnographical museums, which were "perpetuating the old illusion that the important thing is above all a knowledge of material objects" (p. 21), whereas an object merely tricked out with its indigenous name and placed behind glass is devoid of meaning: "our true realm of inquiry is the mechanism of production itself, in other words, of the technical fabrication and the underlying psychic and social conditions of which things in themselves can never be more than withered witnesses, like dried plants in a herbarium" (p. 23).

In short: primacy of the social mechanisms of production (production of material objects as well as of rituals, myths, and beliefs), primacy of the living over the dead, of present over past, of explanation over description—these are the ethnographer's imperatives. They constitute the absolute minimum of equipment essential for any piece of fieldwork, if we take "field" to mean, above all, a state of mind. And in the same article he returns, albeit briefly, to the notion, so unusual in those days, that ethnography has its own field of direct, and "in certain circumstances *experimental*," observation (p. 12, my italics). That field is man, although Van Gennep does not actually explain what the exact nature of this "experimental" method in the sciences of man would be. So we must be content to set this very attractive but alas never developed notion beside a quotation from Lévi-Strauss:

> It can happen that experimentation in anthropology will actually precede both observation and hypothesis. One of the peculiarities of the small societies we study stems from the fact that each one of them, as a result of its relative simplicity and the restricted number of variables required to explain its functioning, constitutes an experiment already performed in advance (*Leçon inaugurale*, p. 22).

A close examination of this period in Van Gennep's work—up until about 1914—leaves one with the impression that he was probably the only true ethnologist in France at the time. Not so much on account of his fieldwork, since that amounted to no more than a few expeditions to Savoy and two short trips to Algeria, but because his point of view, his way of apprehending facts—those of everyday life as well as scientific ones—his judgments, and his theoretical caution are always specifically ethnological, whereas Durkheim and his disciples (including Mauss, albeit to a lesser degree) remained, willy-nilly, sociologists and philosophers, using ethnographical evidence to buttress their own theories. In 1934, in an article entitled "Contribution à la méthodologie du folklore," we find Van Gennep still capable of delivering a passing broadside against the great French sociologist and his school:

> When one thinks that Durkheim and others based universal theories on tribes comprising no more than twenty to a hundred individuals, one is assailed by qualms. In Savoy I have been dealing with three million

people. At that rate I could have invented a hundred universal theories just by concentrating on the exceptions alone (p. 27).

Even though he was at this time concerning himself solely with French folklore, it is clear that Van Gennep had not forgotten the theoretical wrangles of his youth.

FOUR

RITES OF PASSAGE

It has been said that *Les Rites de passage* (1910) forms a link joining the two phases of Van Gennep's work, and it would be hard to imagine a theme more suited to that function. Its author was very attached to the book, as he himself made clear in an article on Frazer's *Golden Bough* (*Religions, moeurs et légendes*, 5:39–40): "I confess sincerely that though I set little store by my other books, my *Rites de passage* is like a part of my own flesh, and was the result of a kind of inner illumination that suddenly dispelled a sort of darkness in which I had been floundering for almost ten years." He had found, in fact, what was to constitute the blueprint on which all his future research into French ethnography was to be based.

The darkness he refers to was the miasma of speculations on all the current problems of the day: totemism, taboos, legends, myths and their relation to rituals, and so on. He was now striking out afresh into a field of no less complexity, but it was the concrete complexity of a total society as observed from outside. And what the observer

sees is a proliferation of heterogeneous groupings: totemic groups, castes, families, professional associations,
churches, age-sets, and so on. The life of the individual in
society, whatever the type of society, consists in moving
successively from one generation to another and from one
occupation to another. Each of these transitions (*passages*)
is marked by ceremonies, and the aim of those ceremonies
is to ensure that the transitions are made successfully.
"Since the object is the same, it is absolutely inevitable that
the means of attaining it should be, if not identical in every
detail, at least analogous" (*Rites de passage*, p. 4). It is not
only the human life that is marked off in this way but also
"cosmic" time, which is humanized by further sets of rituals marking lunations, seasons, solstices, years, and so on.

After this preamble, Van Gennep examines the various
classifications of such rituals already put forward, with the
British anthropological school often playing the role of
front-runner. Four independent categories had been
grouped in pairs: sympathetic and animist rituals, rituals
based on dynamism and those based on contagionism (the
distinguishing criterion between animism and dynamism
being whether the power involved is personified—totem,
God, and so on—or impersonal—*mana*). These categories
were supplemented by a number of functional modalities:
rituals could be direct—if their efficacy was immediate—or
indirect—if they were merely intended to trigger off some
external intervention; they were positive if they were "volitions expressed in action," negative if they were taboos.
This meant that any ritual could belong to four categories
at the same time and that there were sixteen possible
classifications. Van Gennep gives a few examples: the
taboo that prohibits a pregnant woman from eating mulberries for fear the child may bear the mark of the fruit is a
direct, negative, dynamist, contagionist ritual! He himself

confesses that it is sometimes difficult to make out whether a ritual is essentially dynamist or animist, but in general this form of classification seems to him to be legitimate. In one sense, this makes his merit all the greater, for it was in the midst of all this confusion, which every attempt at classification seemed to be making worse, that he proposed a simple heuristic "schema" or model easily and directly applicable to the concrete facts. He begins with the idea of the _ceremonial sequence_. He observes that it is very rare for ceremonies to be described from start to finish and even rarer for them to be studied in relation to one another. His book, therefore, will be an attempt to group together all those "that accompany transitions from one situation to another and from one cosmic or social world to another" (p. 13). He divides these rites of passage, or transition rituals, into rites of separation, threshold rites, and rites of aggregation, for which he also employs the terms preliminary, liminary, and postliminary. Their relative importance varies according to the particular populations and types of ceremony under consideration. We find, for example, that rites of separation are more important in funeral ceremonies than in marriage ceremonies, while in the latter it is aggregation rites that form the essential part. We must not let the simplicity of this schema or model lead us into a simplification of the ceremonial facts themselves, however, since these are often complex and tangled; in fact we should, on the contrary, use it to reduce that complexity to some kind of order. We sometimes observe, for instance, that

> the schema becomes double: this occurs when the central threshold has become wide enough to constitute a separate transitional stage in its own right. For example, betrothal is of course a threshold period between adolescence and marriage; but the transition from

adolescence to betrothal itself involves a specific ceremonial series comprising rites of separation from the threshold, threshold rites, and then rites of aggregation to marriage (p. 14).

Van Gennep then introduces the idea of "the displacement of the sacred." The sacred is not an absolute value but "a value that indicates respective situations." This phrase is none too clear, but the examples he gives make it quite plain what he means. A man living normally among his family and clan exists in the profane; if he goes on a journey and finds himself in a foreign group, then he is living in the sacred. Women, if they are viewed by the society in which they live as vessels of impurity, are thereby placed in the sphere of the sacred in relation to the adult males and also, when pregnant, in relation to other women. "In this way, as one places oneself successively in this or that spot within the society as a whole, there is a displacement of 'magic circles' " (p. 16). Each individual, during the course of his lifetime, thus pivots upon himself from time to time and finds himself facing the sacred instead of the profane or vice versa. These shifts, too, are marked by rites of passage aimed at mitigating any attendant evil and disturbing effects.

This notion of the displacement of the sacred may seem extremely simple, not to say elementary. Despite this simplicity, however, it had never been expressed until this time, even though the concept of the sacred itself had already given rise to a whole spate of ethnological writings. It is similar in nature to the idea of the transition ritual in that, although its use is not, properly speaking, theoretical, once established it became an invaluable way of accounting for certain facts, of rescuing them from the chaos of ethnographical observation and classifying them. There is a temptation to underestimate the value of both notions.

Yet we sometimes find that they can very conveniently
replace a whole theory, an edifice often constructed at the
expense of enormous labor in an effort to reconcile conflict-
ing elements. They therefore represent one of Van Gennep's essential contributions.

In the main body of the book Van Gennep examines
transition rituals classified according to the stages of man's
journey through life: pregnancy and confinement, birth
and childhood, initiation rites, betrothal and marriage, and
funerals. Of these, initiation rites occupy a particularly important place because they are typical and very pure transition rituals. And Van Gennep stresses the fact that they
celebrate the attainment of social, not physical, puberty.
The other rituals are those relating to physical transitions
and to ceremonies marking the arrival of the seasons and
months. These latter are also sympathetic rituals of fertility, multiplication, and growth. Mannhardt, Frazer,
Hoffmann-Krayer, and others had grasped this aspect
clearly enough but, unfortunately, only that aspect, and
such ceremonies are in fact also transition rituals.

This important book was underestimated by other
writers at the time. Marcel Mauss reviewed it for *L'Année
sociologique* (11 [1906–9]:200–202) in fairly uncomplimentary
terms and even with a measure of bad faith. He accuses its
author of seeing nothing but rites of passage everywhere,
of claiming that this "law" (Van Gennep speaks simply of a
"schema") governs all religious representations, that it constitutes the very rhythm of thought itself and the origin of
all philosophies from the Greeks to Nietzsche. On this particular point, all Van Gennep in fact does is to mention the
concept of the eternal return in connection with certain
peoples (he names the Lushei) who view the individual
human life-pattern not as rectilinear but as circular, going
from life to death and from death to life. And although

Mauss does very grudgingly accept the idea of the rite of passage, it is only to tax it with being a truism. He rejects the idea that such rites necessarily contain the sequence laid down by the author: separation, threshold, aggregation. Finally, Mauss accuses the work of the inherent defect of the (British) anthropological school, which is to go wildly galloping off through the whole of history and ethnography instead of bringing analysis to bear on a few typical and accurately studied facts.

The verdict of the French sociological school was thus a harsh one. This lack of understanding was to be mitigated in the following decades, but it is by no means certain that it has been completely dissipated even now. Yet *Les Rites de passage* contains a number of fascinating ideas, despite the drawback of being badly presented and insufficiently developed.

The idea of the rite of passage or transition ritual itself is based on that of the ceremonial (or ritual) sequence. It is perhaps a truism (as Mauss was to claim) to say that a ritual must be performed in order to merit the name of ritual, and performed in accordance with a prescribed sequence of actions.

> The order in which the rituals follow one another and must be performed is already, in itself, a magico-religious element of essential importance. The main purpose of this book is precisely to react against the "folklorist" or "anthropological" method that consists in extracting various rituals, either positive or negative, from a sequence and then considering them in isolation, thereby depriving them of their principal reason for being and their logical situation within that particular set of mechanisms (p. 127).

We must avoid a pitfall here: Van Gennep is concerned at this point not so much with stressing the importance of the ethnographic context, of the "total social fact," as with putting his finger on the very essence of ritual itself, an essence that is valid for social and religious ceremonies just as much as for the private rites of the obsessive individual. To exist at all, a ritual must first and foremost be inscribed in time and space or, rather, be reinscribed, since it is following a prior model given in myth.

Certainly Van Gennep does not go as far as that. But he does return with great persistence at several points in his book to this notion of sequence, and he is convinced of its importance:

> The object of this book is quite different [from that of discovering identical rites performed by diverse peoples]. It is not the rites in their particular details that have captured my interest but rather their essential meaning and their relative situations within ceremonial wholes, their *sequence* . . . ; beneath the multiplicity of forms, whether consciously expressed or merely latent, we always find a sequence type: *the pattern of transition rituals* (p. 275).

Whatever Mauss may have thought, Van Gennep was not claiming to have stated a law but merely to have provided a heuristic and methodological schema, a pattern enabling one to impose an order on the virgin jungle of ethnographic facts.

That was the essential contribution of *Les Rites de passage*. But there are other interesting ideas to be found in it too, even though they have unfortunately been left in the state of uncut diamonds. Every transition ritual contains three successive stages: separation, threshold, aggregation. The discovery of this succession is certainly due to Van Gennep, but he himself stresses again and again the importance of the central, intermediate stage, an importance, he claimed, that no one had as yet perceived. He points out that Hertz, in his "Contribution à une étude sur la représentation collective de la mort" (*L'Année sociologique*, 1907), had alluded to what he called "the transitional state" of the period between marriage and the birth of the first child, which corresponds to a similar stage undergone by the dead in Borneo. But until that point the exclusive concern of ethnologists had been to discover similarities of content among rituals, not similarities of form. These central, threshold periods are sometimes so extensive that they acquire a certain autonomy. Betrothal, for instance, itself a threshold rite, a waiting stage between celibacy and marriage, can sometimes include a further ceremonial sequence of separation, threshold, and aggregation. Van Gennep does not develop this idea any further, contenting himself with stressing its originality, its importance, and its function: "This interpretation makes it easy, for example, to orient ourselves among the complexities of the preliminary rites of marriage and to grasp the underlying reason for their sequences" (*Rites*, p. 275).

Another point emphasized by Van Gennep, the "discovery" of which must be credited to him entirely, concerns the importance of *physical transition* in these rites. This is a point he develops at somewhat greater length, since he devotes the first chapter of his book to it; but he does encounter difficulties in providing a firm theoretical foundation for it, despite the fact that his intuition in the matter is entirely convincing. For him, transition from one social situation to another is identical with physical transition: entry into a village or house, passing from one room to another, passing through streets or public places. This is why the rite of passage is very often expressed physically by passing beneath a gateway or by the opening of doors. Van Gennep adds: "It is rarely that a 'symbol' is involved here; transition as an idea is for the semicivilized a strictly physical transition" (p. 276). And it is certainly true that the various groups making up the total society are, among the "semicivilized," physically separated: children live with the women until a certain age; adolescents sometimes live together at a distance from the married adults; warriors live apart from smiths; the Jews in Europe were enclosed in their ghettos, and so on. "A change in social category implies a change of domicile, a fact expressed by rites of passage in their various forms" (p. 276). We are thus dealing with an expression that is "rarely a symbol" (Van Gennep's own quotation marks). It is in effect clearly evident that the transition ritual is essentially a physical transition; however, in what sense Van Gennep is able to state that it is "rarely a symbol" is difficult to grasp from his text. Presumably he is opposing the physical to the symbolic in the sense that we oppose concrete to abstract, effective to latent, and so on. But it is an idea that would have been worth developing.

We have seen that Van Gennep's discovery of the idea of the transition ritual was not greeted with overmuch enthusiasm by his contemporaries. Even today it is not easy to grasp its full importance, simply because it has entered so completely into ethnologists' vocabulary and practice that they sometimes have no idea who originated it and are no longer able to appreciate its precise function. That function is heuristic in nature. Van Gennep himself was perfectly aware of that fact, even though he did not always state it clearly enough. It is a "schema," he said, a pattern, and as such its function is as a tool for the ordering and classification of concrete facts: "the present systematization is not a pure logical construction, but it accords not only with the facts but also with the tendencies underlying them and with social necessities" (p. 269).

All, or almost all, of Van Gennep's later work was to be a proof of this. *Les Rites de passage* should be seen as marking his own "pivoting" in the direction of ethnography and folklore. It was in fact the "schema" first laid down in this book that was to enable him to introduce order and intelligibility into the complexity, the fragmentation, and the apparent—and disheartening—incoherence of folkloric data. He produced the proof of this without delay: in 1910 he published an article in the *Revue de l'histoire des religions* (6:37–55, 183–217, 322–55) entitled "De quelques rites de passage en Savoie." In it he gives a brief summary of what he called his "sequence method," with reference to the meaning we ought to assign to an aspersion ritual in the marriage ceremony. For him, an aspersion ritual possesses no meaning in itself. He says, in fact, that if we isolate a ritual

> from the ceremonial context we are led to put forward schemas of development external to the reality and constructed *in abstracto*; but by considering each ritual in relation to the place it occupies within each ceremonial sequence, one can succeed in discovering why that ritual, while remaining the same in itself, nevertheless changes its internal meaning according to whether it precedes or follows such and such another ritual. The aspersion ritual possesses no particular meaning in isolation, but it possesses a fertility-giving meaning in marriage rites, or a propitiation meaning in Egyptian childhood ceremonies, during which seeds, peas, or salt are thrown to placate the djinns by "feeding them"; and in other contexts it has a purification meaning, because small seeds are equated with waterdrops; and it can possess many other meanings still, in accordance with the specific magico-religious properties attributed to the objects scattered in different localities (p. 207).

And let us not forget that Van Gennep wrote those words in 1910. On the preceding page we find him firmly dismissing historical interpretation. Aspersion with nuts was also part of the Roman marriage ritual, but that is no reason to see the ceremony in Savoy as a borrowing or a survival. The diffusion of this particular ritual is worldwide, as Mannhardt and Frazer have shown; therefore any historical interpretation is valueless, since the facts as they stand may just as easily be the result of random distribution as of direct filiation. Only replacement of the ritual within an actual ceremonial context can provide meaning.

In the unpublished notes for his intended conclusion to the *Manuel de folklore français contemporain*, written during the last years of his life, Van Gennep is still as convinced as ever of the correctness and the necessity of the transition-ritual model. Although he remains as modest and sober as ever in his mode of expression, his tone is nevertheless striking in its firmness and conviction. This can be judged from the following passage:

> What differs from people to people and from civilization to civilization, in the broad sense of that term, is not therefore the fundamental principles but merely the techniques of execution. We then penetrate into a dense jungle of material whose details seem to be intertwined or heaped up at random until the evidence has been thoroughly sifted and examined. But once that is done, we find the dramatic scenario emerging as clearly as the scenario of any modern play. There is always a beginning (I do not a say a source), a middle, and an end. Nothing could be more obvious. Yet how is it that what is so obvious was not grasped by folklorists much earlier? How is it that they did not attempt to show, by establishing the observed facts in their series, how these ineluctable stages fitted together?

Not only does Van Gennep insist on the pertinence of his sequence pattern, he goes on to apply it to a much broader field of human activities, seeing it as a means of "dramatic" expression:

> I attempted in my *Rites de passage* to show that, throughout the individual human lifetime, or the cycle of the year, or other longer or shorter cyclic periods, it is always the same conditions we find determining expressions that are not only parallel but that, above all, succeed one another always and everywhere, whatever the period of civilization examined, in a certain order. I tried to show also that this order is immanent in things themselves, in other words, in the relations that link individuals one to another and to their type of society. For simplicity's sake I called this necessity the law of sequences. It is expressed in certain cases by rituals, in others by poetry, music, and even, in a sense, by painting and sculpture. One can go from the simple to the complex, or vice versa: the problem remains the same. What we have to do is to classify an individual within his environment, or suggest to the spectator the series of emotions intended.

He had already tackled this problem of the dramatization of narratives as early as 1910 in *La Formation des légendes* (see p. 51, above): certain rites enact myths that are in a way scenarios. Van Gennep then went on to give a brief sketch of the development of what we may call the drama (in a sense close to that of the word in Greek) from initiation rites and mystery plays through to the theater of today. It was not, of course, his purpose, but there is room for regret that he should have remained content to indicate the possible applications of this law of sequences in so sparse and sporadic a way.

FIVE

THE METHODOLOGY OF
FOLKLORE

As I have said, we may take the 1914–18 war as an approximate and convenient line of demarcation between Van
Gennep's ethnological works proper and the preoccupation with folklore that was soon to become exclusive. All
the same, it is artificial to draw an arbitrary line of this sort
in any man's career, and in fact Van Gennep had become
interested in French ethnography very early on, during the
time when he was still working on general theories. He
was in fact sending out questionnaires on the folklore of
Auvergne and the Velay as early as 1909, while at the same
time personally undertaking a direct investigation in
Savoy. It is nevertheless beyond dispute that, after the
publication of *L'Etat actuel du problème totémique* in 1920, he
abandoned his studies of the general problems of ethnology in order to apply himself exclusively to the ethnography of France. This period in fact coincides with an
extreme "low" in French ethnology and sociology, which
had suffered heavy losses as a result of the war: a number
of the younger generation just beginning to publish prom-

ising work had fallen victim to it, among them Robert
Hertz, Maxime David, Antoine Bianconi, Jean Reynier,
and Henri Beuchat.

It was to be several years before Marcel Mauss would
succeed in training a new generation of ethnologists, and it
was in this near vacuum that Van Gennep decided to devote himself definitively and wholeheartedly to French
ethnography, a field even more deserted than that of traditional ethnology. The nineteenth and early twentieth
centuries had in fact seen a great deal of zeal deployed in
the field by collectors, local savants, hobbyists, and provincial notables, but often in a muddled way and employing an approach vitiated by what Van Gennep called "that
psychic and methodological malady": the historical
method. As a result, ethnography in France badly lacked
both working methods and scientific frameworks for
classifying and organizing the mass of data already collected. Van Gennep provided them. And at the same time
he instituted methods of gathering living data: collection
and notation.

In 1924 he published a slim volume called *Le Folklore*, in
which he examines the history, the object, and the
methods of folklore. That is the term he uses, for back in
1914 he had already freed it from its accumulated burden of
misunderstanding when he wrote: "folklore is the ethnography of European rural populations, nothing else"
(*Religions, moeurs et légendes*, 5:19). Early folklorists had
concerned themselves in the first place with fairy stories
and other supernatural tales but later came to realize that
this material contained vestiges of earlier beliefs and ways,
which they then included in their field of study. A further
broadening of the subject brought in legends of saints,
folk songs, ceremonies, art, and so on. In practice, the domain of folklore is one specific element of social life: the

popular (or folk) element. Its productions are in a sense
collective. For instance, one can establish a distinction between works produced by the "higher" literature, of which
the authors are known, and a region's anonymous tales,
legends, and myths. Despite the fact that they have no
known author, however, these latter are nevertheless not
collective creations. A folk production is certainly created
with the help of general, common, and collective
constituent elements, but it is nonetheless the work of an
individual. Very rarely is any trace of him found, though it
is sometimes possible to discover the source of the particular set of collective elements on which he has drawn. "For
the essential problem, in folklore as in the other branches
of sociology, is to determine with the greatest possible
precision, in each specific case, the relation between the
individual and the mass" (*Le Folklore*, p. 25). Invention and
even transformation are individual phenomena. The
authors of collective productions remain for the most part
anonymous and unknown. One can sometimes assign
them approximately to a particular time and place. For
instance, Van Gennep places the inventor of the screw
principle early in the Second Iron Age and in the Cham-
pagne district. This was a truly collective folk invention,
for, since its mechanism is both simple and easily applicable, it very rapidly became a common possession.

Clearly, Van Gennep's doctrine on this point has
remained the same: folk productions are not collective, and
to say of certain elements that they are common and collective is not the same thing as saying that they have been
collectively invented.

The second point on which he remains equally firm concerns the relationship between folklore and history.
Folklore may have to concern itself with data from the past,
but it does so solely in order to discover the antecedents of

some present or even "nascent" datum (see above, p. 37); for the domain of folklore is the living, and in this sense it is a biological science. Although he rejects history, Van Gennep does, nevertheless, need a diachronic process, and he turns to collective psychology to provide him with its mode of operation. It is customs, he says, the study of which falls within the domain of folklore, that form "the true links of that 'chain of tradition' constituting the constant element in national life viewed as a whole" (pp. 28–29). Here again he does not develop his idea further, presumably because he lacked the convenient tool later provided by the synchronic/diachronic antithesis.

The field of folklore does not encompass all social groups; it is concerned with peasants, rural life, and any vestiges of the latter that may persist in urban environments. In his *Manuel de folklore contemporain* (vol. 1, pt. 1, pp. 54–55) Van Gennep qualifies this distinction somewhat.[2] There is no doubt that customs and traditions show greater persistence in country districts than they do in towns. Nevertheless, there does exist a specifically urban folklore, even though it is more difficult to observe and is confined to specific social categories, particularly the workers and petite bourgeoisie. Since the environment in which it originated was so very different—as indeed are its aims and forms—it is impossible to put it on the same footing with rural folklore. The latter in fact plays a role of social cohesion, and this is not the case with urban folklore, which is found only in scattered fragments—in what Sébillot called "crumbs." Van Gennep leads his readers to suppose that this unorganized quality derives from the intrinsic nature of urban folklore itself, but he does not really commit himself clearly on this point; the most credible hypothesis explains this fragmentary aspect as the result of decadence and disappearances. In his

Manuel Van Gennep supplements the rural environment
with the maritime environment (the folklore of fishermen
in particular) and the folklore of schoolchildren, conscripts,
and regular soldiers. He also records as an observed fact
that women seem more given to knowing and preserving
folk traditions than men, but he is unwilling to state this as
a general law.

Before tackling the methodological problems involved,
Van Gennep lists in his little book *Le Folklore* the fields to
which the term can be applied.

> The domain I assign to folklore here is much more ex-
> tensive than that accepted by the early "traditionists,"
> who restricted the field of "transmission by tradition"
> to folktales and legends, songs, beliefs and obser-
> vances, witchcraft, and such like. The progress of our
> science has since obliged us to add the study of all
> ceremonies, games and dances, folk cults to saints,
> home and village life, household utensils, tools of all
> sorts, minor and major arts, institutions created by the
> people or surviving from former eras, and, lastly, ways
> of feeling and modes of expression that differentiated
> the "popular" from the "higher."

He then adds: "parallel to this, our methods have become
both more far-reaching and more precise" (pp. 30–31).

What are these methods? And in what way do they differ from those of ethnography as Van Gennep defined
them in the earlier phase of his work?

Pride of place goes to the method of observation, since
folklore is concerned with living, present-day facts. The
historical method serves to determine the antecedents of
those facts, but, once again, Van Gennep warns against
the historical "mania," since the attitude of the folklorist is
diametrically opposed to that of the historian. This attitude
requires a "psychic displacement" aimed precisely at evad-

ing the pull of historicism. The position of folklore in relation to history is consequently very ambiguous: folklore is
concerned solely with present-day, living facts, yet it is
also trying to replace those facts in the "chain of tradition."
It must therefore find the antecedents that will provide the
previous links in that chain, and the folklorist, although he
does not know what the future links will be, does know
that there will in fact be such links—that the chain will
continue. "Thus folklore produces a feeling that the observed facts contain the seeds of future possibilities,
whereas the historical fact makes one feel that all its possibilities have already been expressed" (*Le Folklore*, p. 35).
The material of the folklorist is the living, and the living
has by definition not only a past but also a future. In other
words, every folkloric fact contains a static element and a
dynamic element. Seen from this viewpoint, "the multiplicity of forms, and of the factors involved (or of the
causes, if you prefer), far from being an encumbrance or an
obstacle, are the source of higher intellectual pleasure, the
pleasure that consists in using reason and knowledge to
bring order into seeming chaos" (p. 36). Hence the defec-
tiveness of the work carried out by early folklorists (and
even by Van Gennep's contemporaries, since Sébillot is
named), who contented themselves with collecting curious
facts because they regarded them simply as survivals, as
lifeless accretions left over from past ages. For Van Gennep, the subject most closely related to folklore is linguistics, and here again we see the full extent of his modernity
as a thinker. For linguists, he tells us, "know that every
language, however general or specialized, is in an incessant state of transformation" (p. 38). It is true that he
does not go so far as to suppose that sociocultural transformations occur, in a sense, in accordance with the same
model as linguistic transformations. He simply notes the

theoretical interest taken by linguists in folklore and the practical interest displayed by folklorists in linguistics, particularly in the study of dialects.

The other methodological tool of the folklorist is the comparative method. Van Gennep adds nothing new here to his earlier account of this method (see above, pp. 38 ff.) apart from a warning: we must not simply compare things at random; it is permissible only to compare facts within the same category. Then, without apparently making any distinction between the theoretical and practical fields, he lists the techniques available to the folklorist: direct personal investigation, questionnaires, and cartography. These matters were to be developed at greater length in the later *Manuel*.

Van Gennep does, however, reveal one new preoccupation in *Le Folklore*. This concerns the classification of the data collected, and it stems from his experiences in the preparation and subsequent execution of his own investigations in various parts of France. The folklorist should concern himself, he tells us, not merely with classifying the collected evidence but also with acquiring a knowledge of the "frameworks" employed by earlier researchers. In this way he will not only come to observe facts more accurately but will also learn how to extract more information from them. The nature of social facts governs the nature of the framework most appropriate to them. They present themselves as "volumes with facets"; to describe them, one must examine each of the facets successively and in a particular order: "One may begin where one wishes; but subsequently that order must be adhered to" (p. 46). The listing of these facets is what Van Gennep terms the "framework," and he examines three examples: that of Paul Sébillot's *Folklore de France*, that of the *Manual of the English Folklore Society*, and that of Hoffmann-Krayer's *Bi-*

bliographie folklorique. All three present defects, but the last has the merit of being the most complete and, above all, the most flexible, enabling one to accommodate any modifications that the material may subsequently make necessary. "One must always, as far as is possible, allow oneself to be guided by the observed reality and regard scientific classification as no more than a filing cabinet to be enlarged and improved on as new needs arise. This is why I have not used the word *classification* here, but only the term *framework*" (p. 51). Here again Van Gennep's empiricism has the last word.

This slender volume marks an important stage in Van Gennep's work. It shows that at this point he had already perfected the methodology that was to ensure the success not only of his monographs devoted to various French provinces—the Dauphiné (1932–33), Burgundy (1934), Flanders and Hainaut (1935), Auvergne and Velay (1942)—but also of his later *Manuel de folklore français contemporain*, which covers not only the whole domain of French folklore but also the discipline's theoretical and methodological problems.

Three of these monographs were brought out by the publishing house of Maisonneuve in a series entitled Contributions to the Folklore of the French Provinces, a series launched by Van Gennep himself and intended, he tells us, not to provide a complete study of each individual region but to "situate already collected but as yet unpublished data in their correct categories while adding a comparative commentary and also, in certain cases, crosschecking them historically." He refused to make the books into individual, self-contained works: the all-important thing to him was to construct the frameworks within which the material collected was to be inserted, since the material itself is infinite and the quest for it open-ended, for the simple reason that folklore studies are concerned with the living, and the living is ceaselessly renewing itself.

These monographs all conform to an identical plan of presentation, which was also to be that used in the *Manuel de folklore français contemporain*, though that, of course, was unhappily never completed, on account of the author's death. After a preamble dealing with the methods of fact-gathering employed (direct investigation, questionnaires) and an account of earlier research in the field, we come to the first section proper, which deals with the stages of the individual human life. The second part deals with periodic ceremonies. Both these sections employ the theoretical schema laid down in *Les Rites de passage*. Then come folk cults of saints, folk medicine and witchcraft, folk literature, and games, and the size—and even the presence or absence—of each of these chapters is a function of that particular region's specific character and of the evidence available. It will be apparent that the ground covered by these monographs does not coincide exactly with the field that Van Gennep had assigned to folklore in his book of that name (see above, p. 71). Specifically, they lack any examination of tools, utensils, techniques, or the arts, even though Van Gennep had earlier proved himself an excellent technologist with his study of Kabyle pottery in Algeria. However, we have already noted his great distrust of material objects, which he referred to once as "withered witnesses," as well as his preference for what were to him the much more interesting processes of psychic production and creation (see above, p. 55).

It is in his *Le Folklore* of 1924 that Van Gennep justifies the application of his rites-of-passage schema to the ethnography of rural societies. The ceremonies that mark the stages in an individual's life and in the cycle of the year are "always concerned with the transition from one stage or phase to another and are all constituted on one and the same plan, following a more or less simple and rectilinear pattern" (p. 90). As his example he takes marriage ceremonies, the aim of which is to unite two individuals and two families or well-defined groups which, from a previous state of separation, move progressively closer together until they merge to form a new "cell." This schema is found among all the world's populations: "What differ are the forms, the details, the symbols, but not the internal armature" (ibid.). In France, and the rural societies of the West generally, these transition rituals present a considerable degree of complexity as a result of the ascendancy achieved by the Christian religion. In the simplest cases we find purely religious ceremonies on the one hand and purely profane ceremonies on the other. Thus the majority of pre-Christian agrarian rites have been inserted into the religious calendar—for example, those marking the summer and winter solstices have in all probability been transposed into the feasts of Saint John the Baptist (Midsummer Day) and Christmas—but elsewhere we may still find purely profane agricultural rituals, such as the still extant custom, found almost throughout France, of preserving the last sheaf of each year's harvest until the next year, sometimes ornamenting it with ribbons. Most of the time, however, the ceremonial sequences display a mixture of Christian elements with other elements that may be referred to as profane, pre-Christian, or pagan. Certain regions have preserved the custom of a funeral meal shared by all the members of the family after the burial, a custom that existed among the ancient Romans and has no connection at all with Christianity, even though the preceding funeral service and burial ceremony themselves are Christian.

Agrarian rituals were integrated into the ceremonies of

the church very early and have retained their seasonal character: the spring cycle was incorporated into the Lent and Easter ceremonies, the summer cycle into those of Saint John and Ascension, the winter cycle into the Twelve Days (between Christmas and Epiphany). But the assimilation was not always total, and a great many marginal elements persisted outside the Christian framework.

Where folk beliefs are concerned, Van Gennep's position is somewhat indecisive at this period. These beliefs are expressed in ceremonies and are for the most part Christian adaptations of prehistoric beliefs. Those that were not given a coat of Christian varnish were opposed by the church; when practiced, they were condemned as magic and witchcraft. The latter comprises more than mere survivals: "It is a field in which, on the contrary, we observe a high degree of technical invention during medieval times, and a strong tendency toward the creation of a genuine science forming part of orthodox Christianity" (p. 92). This medieval system disintegrated during later centuries, however, and there is nothing left of it today but a "scattered dust of evidence."

In Van Gennep's eyes there is no difference between magic and religion as far as their psychic mechanism and procedures are concerned. Their fundamental principles are as follows: the virtue of contact, identification by absorption, direct power of speech (charms, incantations, spells), belief in the action of like on like and contrary on contrary, simple or complex symbolism, and, above all, reasoning by analogy.

Between this tiny volume on folklore and the unfinished monument constituted by the *Manuel de folklore français contemporain* there occurred, as we have seen, the monographs that Van Gennep devoted to various French regions. These enabled him first and foremost to put the frameworks and research techniques he had evolved into practice and to check their validity. Second, these works obliged him to build up a considerable fund of factual evidence with the help of a variety of methods: collation and cross-checking of material already published, direct or firsthand investigation, distribution of wide-spectrum questionnaires, clarification of previously ambiguous details, and the filling-in of gaps. He took particular care over the provision of geographical indications, for a French canton often coincides with a former collective psychic unit, and one may well observe variants in beliefs and ways when crossing the boundary between one of these small territories and the next. He also became even more cautious in his interpretations; in particular, he was by now mistrustful of blanket explanation by pre-Christian survival, whereas earlier he had advanced it without qualms to account for non-Christian elements in a given religious ceremony. He had since come to feel that it cannot be employed unless there is solid evidence to support it. In addition, one sometimes finds that one and the same ritual can be interpreted in a variety of ways. It is essential, he now said, to analyze not just the generalities but also the "specific concomitants," though he did not define this term very clearly. Presumably he was referring to a generalization of his sequence method in the study of rituals or of thematic cycles in the case of oral literature (see above, pp. 42–45). He borrows a comparison from medicine: if a patient has a high fever, the physician cannot immediately determine the infection involved; he has to wait until further "concomitant" symptoms declare themselves in order for a clear clinical picture to emerge: malaria, typhoid, scarlatina, or whatever. "As long as the concomitants are lacking, one must reserve one's diagnosis and simply present the facts as they are given, while

indicating that on the basis of comparative evidence derived from elsewhere—and often from very remote areas
—several interpretations are possible" (*Le Folklore de la
Flandre et du Hainaut français* [1935], preface, p. 10). From
this one can gauge how far Van Gennep has retreated from
the comparative method he was advocating between 1904
and 1914.

SIX

THE *MANUEL* OF CONTEMPORARY
FRENCH FOLKLORE

The aim of Van Gennep's vast though unfinished *Le Manuel de folklore français contemporain* was, according to its author, not simply to present and classify known or fresh material but also "to provide future researchers with general notions on the internal meaning of folklore, its place among the other sciences of man, its methods of observation and interpretation, and its future possibilities" (Preface to vol. 1, p. vi). I need hardly say that no such treatise dealing with France had existed before. This meant that it was necessary "in every province and every direction to return to the original documentary sources, take each tiny fact individually, make a close study of the relations between them, and concentrate on those relations much more than on the facts themselves" (pp. ix–x). Van Gennep is insistent upon this idea of interrelation, for two pages further on he writes: "*Le Manuel* views facts not in isolation but in terms of their psychic and social relations. . . . Even when those relations are not expressly indicated, they exist deep below the surface; the reader is

asked to bear clearly in mind that this *substratum*, to speak
pedantically, constitutes the very essence of the
phenomena under examination" (p. xi). No doubt these
theoretical premises are not expressed in very clear terms.
Presumably we are meant to take them as an expression of
Van Gennep's concern never to isolate a fact from the
sociocultural context that alone can provide it with a meaning. This *substratum* can then be understood as being
composed of the complex networks formed by all the inter-
relations of the various phenomena, one with another, and
the reader is asked not to take the demarcations rendered
necessary by the author's presentation of the facts for dis-
junctions between the phenomena themselves.

Since the order of the *Manuel* is not very clear, it is probably necessary to explain its underlying structure. It was to
consist of four volumes, the second of which never appeared. The third and fourth volumes were published first,
in 1937 and 1938, respectively, and they comprise a series
of questionnaires, a list of provinces and districts, and then
a critical and systematic bibliography, followed by an index
of provinces and authors' names. Between 1943 and 1958
there appeared six further sections, or parts, together making up volume one and devoted to the rituals of the individual life-cycle and the cyclical seasonal ceremonies; the
last of these parts, dealing with the Twelve Days of
Christmas cycle, was published posthumously. The plan of
the bibliography is the same as that adopted in the *Manuel*
itself. It is therefore possible to assess the gaps in the latter
left by the author's death. Volume 2 was to have dealt with
the following subjects: fixed-date ceremonies and
variable-date ceremonies; the cult of the Virgin and the
saints; nature lore (sky, earth, water, flora, fauna, human
body); magic, witchcraft, folk medicine; supernatural beings; shifting and fixed folk literature; music and song;

games, toys, and pastimes; social and juridical folklore; domestic folklore; and folk arts. The project was inordinately ambitious and probably impossible of achievement. We must be grateful that Van Gennep was able to complete the most original and freshest part of it, which deals with those areas most neglected by earlier folklorists.

Van Gennep lays great stress on the fact that his work is a manual and not a descriptive treatise. This means that it offers us a number of working tools: a systematic bibliography, classified according to themes and geographical location; examples of questionnaires devised for use in the field; and practical methods of classifying and notating the material collected. Where the theoretical aspect of folklore is concerned, the general framework put forward by the author makes it possible to integrate any freshly discovered fact into it, and it also reveals the gaps left by earlier researchers, thus making it possible to direct present-day research with a view to filling them.

Volume 1 is prefaced by a long theoretical introduction that confirms most of the principles stated in *Le Folklore* but setting them out at greater length. This introduction bears witness to the maturity of a researcher by now experienced in practical fieldwork. Let us now try to assess how far its author has come since 1924.

Before defining what folklore is, Van Gennep examines the names that have been used to denote the subject down through the years, and he assesses the advantages and drawbacks of each. As we know, the term "folklore" was invented in 1846 by the Englishman W. J. Thoms to replace earlier phrases, usually implying pejorative value judgments, such as "popular antiquities" or "vulgar and common errors" in Britain and *superstitions* in France. The neutrality of "folklore" is not however exempt from ambiguity: if "folk" means "the people" and "lore" means

"learning," the question arises, and Van Gennep did not
fail to ask it, whether this learning is what we have learned
about the folk or what the folk have learned about nature
and the world. His verdict is that it is in the second sense
that we must understand Sébillot's title *Le Folklore de
France*, since it gives an account of "popular"—in the sense
of "of the people"—ideas about the sky, the earth, the sea,
about rivers, plants, animals, and history. But as for his
own practice, Van Gennep tells us that he employs the
term in its first sense: "study, knowledge, science of the
people." Certain German folklorists attempted to make the
same distinction by using the two terms *Volkskunde* and
Volkslehre. Theoretically this problem is not in fact the piece
of hair-splitting it may at first sight appear. The material of
folklore does in fact constitute a body of learning in the
strict sense of that word. But to set it up as an antithesis of
science, as has often been done, and to attempt to prove
that the two have been governed in their development by
diametrically opposed kinds of reason lead to nothing but
dead ends.

In practice it is of little importance whether or not Van
Gennep refuses to accept that the material he collected
possesses the status of learning, since he acts in practice as
though it does.

Despite a slight show of reluctance, he does, however,
accept the term folklore; all the French terms present even
greater disadvantages and, besides, "the English language
has borrowed so many words from us, from the Norman
Conquest down to the middle of the seventeenth century,
that we can repay a little of the compliment now." By now,
too, Van Gennep is no longer protesting against the traditional use of "ethnography" (ethnology) to mean the
study of exotic, primitive, non-European, technologically
simple peoples—take your pick—and "folklore" to mean

the study of present-day rural populations in Europe. In 1911 (*Titres et travaux*, p. 9) he had denounced this illogicality roundly, noting that the Russians alone had ignored this distinction as futile, "since in their country it stares one in the face that a science cannot go changing its name according to whether it is dealing with the Russian peasant or the Finnish, or Crimean, or Tartar peasant, simply because they differ in racial type and language." Thirty years later he has implicitly accepted the reality that underlies this division between folklore and ethnography, since any state of fact that can persist so long, despite its surface absurdity, has acquired a legal right to existence, even though it is difficult to determine its causes precisely.

Before defining the thing itself, however, he beats its bounds, as it were, and in doing so makes it clear that, although very expansionist in theory, he knows how to bow before reality. The whole of linguistics—phonetics, morphology, syntax, and semantics—ought to belong within the realm of folklore, "since it deals with collective folk phenomena." And whereas the study of techniques, crafts, and tools still formed part of folklore in the eighteenth century, the next century, bringing, as it did, vast industrial expansion, swept folklore aside in order to constitute the new discipline of political economy. During the same period folklore was also held in contempt by history (as far as contemporary material was concerned). The study of religions, however, still retains close and inevitable links with folklore: "there is not one of my sections, even the specifically technological section, that does not, at some moment or other of industrial and collective life, display the action of belief or the association of technical activities with other activities based on a particular belief" (*Manuel*, p. 15). Moreover, psychology has made progress, thanks to the comparative method. Van Gennep is thinking here of Lévy-Bruhl and accepting his thesis that the folk mentality is differentiated from the scientific mentality by its use of reasoning by analogy and reasoning by participation. As for human geography, which overlaps folklore to a certain extent, it is mistaken in taking the earth as its starting point, since it is man that is the essential factor, while soil and climate constitute no more than secondary factors. Sociology, on the other hand, has the closest links of all with folklore, "so much so that, all things considered . . . we must look upon the science of ways and customs as belonging wholly to sociology" (p. 19). Another young science, sexology, must also be linked to folklore, since it is clear that betrothal and marriage ceremonies, fertility rites, and certain practices of folk medicine fall to some extent within its field.[1]

In order to characterize folklore positively, Van Gennep begins by saying that it is a biological science, since its object of study is a living being. This is not a new idea in his work (see above, pp. 15–16), but in the *Manuel* he clears up the misapprehension created by certain critics who had understood his earlier remarks in a transformist or evolutionist sense. In his eyes, the term biology simply means "that which deals with life." In fact, we have already seen on several occasions that the word was for Van Gennep a means of contrasting the study of living data with that of dead, or in other words past, facts, and of distinguishing the biological method from the historical method. He stresses this distinction again here:

> I am not dealing here with a theory or a system but with an *angle of observation* that leads us to see the facts of folklore and ethnography in a quite different light from that shed on them by the mechanistic viewpoint or the historical viewpoint and that enables us to subordinate the thousands of superficial morphological

details to the study of living agents and social functions.
It also enables us to cease viewing the multiplicity of
variations in detail throughout time and space as an aber-
ration or difficulty and to see it instead as an ineluc-
table norm, as the expression of those general laws that
it is our science's aim to formulate with a flexibility
corresponding to real present-day biological conditions
(*Manuel*, p. 20).

This position is not new in his work. The fact of regarding the object of folklore as being constituted by living
phenomena cannot give rise to any preformulated theory
or to dogmatic preconceptions. He himself is concerned to
stress this: it is an *angle of observation*. This means that he
gives pride of place to the gathering of living data, in other
words, facts as contemporary and living factors, thereby
excluding the historical and mechanistic "angles." He perceives two advantages in this. First, it is possible in this
way to capture and harness the multiplicity of the details as
they appear to the observer, since the latter knows that
they are the consequence of dynamic social factors.
Second, the observer is likewise able to harness the variations that appear in different times and places without
being obliged to treat them as anomalies: laws exist, laws
that must be discerned from a perusal of the contemporary
facts and that will make it possible to integrate earlier facts
into a coherent process. To employ a more up-to-date terminology, it is a question of reducing superficially incoher-
ent diachronic data to order by means of synchronic social
processes. And indeed, those processes, by the very fact
that they exist and function, cannot be subject to the
whims of chance.

Although Van Gennep does not explicitly say so or even
imply it, we can recognize here the entire problematics of
Saussurian linguistics. For Saussure, in the same way, the

synchronic relations of a language can and must be defined
without any recourse to history, while a language's diachronic (historical) processes, on the other hand, can be
clarified by using its synchronic processes as a filter. To be
truthful, this corollary does go a little beyond Saussure's
own thought. According to Ducrot and Todorov,[2] he
seems to suggest, rather, that diachronic processes ought
to be studied in isolation from all synchronic considerations. But linguists today, affirming the primacy of the
synchronic over the diachronic even more strongly where
the interpretation of the facts is concerned, are attempting
to base their diachronic studies on our knowledge of a
language's synchronic states.

There is no evidence that Van Gennep had read Saussure's *Cours de linguistique générale*, which was published in
1916, and he does not mention it in the bibliography to his
Manuel. And although he certainly regarded linguistics as a
discipline very closely akin to folklore, he was referring,
when he talked of linguistics, to schools of thought far
removed from that of Saussure: the school that concerns
itself with the changing meaning of words (lexicography);
that which studies the relations between words and things
(Gilliéron's linguistic atlases); and lastly the onomastic
school typified by Dauzat, which studied the names of
places and people. We are forced to conclude that this was
a phenomenon of simultaneous invention, that both men
arrived simultaneously at a formula that had become
necessary at a certain moment in the development of the
social sciences. Yet Saussure's discovery alone had direct
influence on those sciences. What Van Gennep had been
proclaiming since 1908 was not heard and so made no
more than what one might call a subterranean contribution
to the development of structuralism, either in linguistics or
ethnology.

French folklorists had always given the idea of oral tradition and transmission the central role in their definition of the discipline. Van Gennep examines a few of these definitions, not uncritically, but does not at first offer one of his own. He remarks that "all the attempts that have been made, in various countries, to constrict our science and its definition within excessively strict frameworks have failed" (*Manuel*, p. 40). Though he does not say so, the reason for this attitude is probably that he has no wish to give such a definition himself. He prefers to employ what one might call a "diffuse" method. Having concluded a first stage, which consisted in outlining the field of folklore by establishing its kinship with the disciplines closest to it and in giving an account of its history, he then attempts to define what he calls "the environments of folklore," by which he means those social areas in which it is possible to observe the formation, development, degeneration, and transmission of folkloric phenomena. These environments make up the "people." But what is the people, or folk? For some, the term is synonymous with the whole nation, for others it means "the vulgar." Van Gennep resolves the problem elegantly, if not rigorously:

For scientists, the difficulty of attributing a fact or series of folkloric facts to the people is lessened by a sort of intuition, something acquired only by cultivating a particular science methodically and over a long period, just as the numismatist eventually acquires the power to differentiate by touch, from the soapy or rough sensation against his fingertips, between genuine coins and counterfeits. In the same way, a folklorist can differentiate quite easily between a genuine folk song, one that belongs to the people's own treasure hoard, and those that had their origin in wine-cellars or café-concerts, however widely they may be sung in the countryside (p. 42).

It is amusing to note this comparison with numismatics when we remember that Van Gennep began his scientific career by collecting all the "old pennies" he could lay his hands on and that his first published works were concerned with the coinage of the dukes of Savoy. All folklorists will in fact testify to having experienced this intuition. Once again we find that Van Gennep is refusing to hand on a dogmatic and ready-made methodology, knowing as he does that anything of the sort would be both futile and dangerous. And, on the other hand, he is concerned to stress the value of intuition, which is based not on an uncontrolled and uncontrollable irrationality but on long practical experience that has engendered a certain knowledge. Nevertheless, he does give an approximate definition of the term "popular." In the *Manuel* he employs it in two of the three senses ratified by current usage: first, that which has been created by the people or had its origin among the people; second, that which is ordinarily to be found among the people, even though it may be aristocratic or middle-class in origin. However, he does reject the third meaning—"coarse, brutal, illogical"—as vitiated by its inherent value judgment. In cases where the origin of phenomena can be established with certainty, it is better to make a distinction between the "popular" and the "popularized." Some schools of thought would like to eliminate from folklore anything that did not originate within the people. That is Coirault's position when he states, with reference to folk songs: "Everything that is folklore is popular; but everything that is popular is not necessarily folklore." The German and Swiss schools, on the other hand, apply the term folklore to everything that has currency in a society's popular strata (whether consciously or unconsciously, Hoffmann-Krayer says); this is what they mean by *Volksgut*, the folk's or people's wealth, its property, its learning. They see it as desirable that one should be able to establish both the source environment and the use environment of every folkloric phenomenon. If Van Gennep does not declare allegiance to either of these two schools of thought, it is because he is only too well aware of the practical difficulties this kind of research presents. It presupposes, in fact, "a specific gift of creation specific to the people or the collectivity as such; a perfect knowledge of the paths and agents of transmission from individual to collectivity and vice versa; and finally a profound acquaintance with the folklore of the entire area under examination" (p. 44).

As to this last point, it need hardly be stressed how far the gaps in our knowledge of French folklore exceed the areas of knowledge themselves. The paths of transmission have been studied, but the mechanism of that transmission still remains somewhat mysterious. These days, Van Gennep says, it is accepted that folk transmission is strictly oral, as opposed to the use of writing in learned transmission. But this cliché is one that "better-conducted" investigations have partly undermined. One does in fact find written compilations, made by singers or healers, for example, that have been passed on from generation to generation within a single family. Moreover, the printing press can intervene in the process; it has been possible to establish, for instance, that certain formulas used by healers in their spells were derived from printed books circulated by peddlers, the texts of which were then subjected to alterations and interpolations. Books of magic like the *Grand Albert* and the *Petit Albert*, although in fact printed, circulated exclusively among the people. For Van Gennep, in consequence, the criterion is not so much whether transmission was oral or written as in what social environment it took place. And the individual-versus-collective criterion is equally inefficacious. Van Gennep had earlier protested vigorously (cf. p. 47, above) against

the equation of the popular with the collective, pointing
out that the individual alone is capable of creation and that
all so-called collective productions have merely been
adopted by the collectivity. In his *Manuel* he softens his
position somewhat. The romantic conception according to
which the people as such is capable of creation is seen,
from the sociological point of view, as possessing a certain
element of truth. For an individual cannot, in fact, modify
an existing social state single-handed or impose innova-
tions upon it; he is obliged to act upon a very small group,
which in its turn draws in other groups, so that, by a process of agglomeration, an entire stratum will adopt the
innovation or social modification. In practice such an
occurrence is fairly rare; the most common situation is that
of a status quo that forces one to adopt "the theory of the
subconscious and of a psychic and corporeal automatism
as the ultimate foundations of tradition" (p. 52). This is
why it is essential to retain the terms "tradition" and "traditional," which enable us to express the force of inertia
and resistance to change observed in folkloric phenomena.

After reading these pages aimed at outlining the frontiers of the science of folklore, the reader may be disap-
pointed by the absence of any definition of it in the strict
sense of the word. But if he has been really attentive, he
will have derived from what he has been offered a benefit
much more important than any definition could provide.
He has been offered the results of long and intelligent experience, an experience impregnated with a true sympathy
for its object of study. This will not absolve the tyro
researcher from submitting himself to the same practical
experience, but it will help him avoid the mistakes, blun-
ders, dead ends, and prejudices that were the lot of many
of his predecessors.

In his chapters on the interpretation of folkloric material
Van Gennep preserves the same caution and the same em-

piricism. For a long while the facts of folklore were interpreted as survivals, and Van Gennep saw this as the result
of applying nineteenth-century evolutionism and belief in
progress to the subject, an attitude Sébillot had still not
shaken off when he entitled one of his books *Le Paganisme
contemporain chez les peuples celto-Latins* (Paris: Doin, 1908).
It is undeniable that survivals do exist, particularly in rituals and the physical form of objects. But the application of
this principle to all folkloric productions presupposes a
value judgment: anteriority is being inherently coupled
with intellectual inferiority. The participationist mode of
thought is neither anterior nor inferior to logical thought:

> In reality, man has always and everywhere thought in
> two ways, and we continue to employ both today, at
> different times and according to particular circum-
> stances. These two modes of reasoning and drawing
> conclusions, and the two modes of action consequent
> upon them, are thus both equally normal and con-
> stituent elements of the thought of the entire human
> species (p. 97).

Another theory, that of degeneration, which presupposed
the gradual breaking-down of an earlier and coherent system, had by then lost all support. Yet it can be verified in
certain limited cases. As with the survival theory, it is simply wrong to view it as "the key that opens every door."

There are other theories in the field of folklore, but they
are applicable only to particular categories of facts, and
Van Gennep's intention was to examine them in the
chapters of the *Manuel* dealing specifically with those
categories. In the event, this intention was to bear fruit
only in the section, or part, dealing with the individual
human life, "Du Berceau à la tombe" (From Cradle to
Grave), where it is his own theory of transition rituals that
is involved. The other sections remained unrealized, as did

his plan to expound in them the theories concerning the origin of folktales, the relationship between popular cults and magic and religion, and the ethnic origin of house styles. In this introduction he goes no further than saying that these theories are all based on the comparative or ethnographic method, "the use of which is now not only accepted, despite the opposition...of the historians, but regarded as normal and even essential" (p. 98). Those were thus his last words on the subject.

Empiricist though he was, Van Gennep nevertheless states quite clearly that it is impossible to observe anything without having some theory or hypothesis in mind during the course of one's actual investigation, since, "in order to find, one must know what one is looking for" (p. 99). The raw datum signifies nothing; in order to isolate its meaning, one must search for its "concomitants" (see above, p. 81). Having examined all the possible theoretical attitudes that folklore can adopt with regard to its data (psychological, economic, geographical, ethnic, orographic, geological, linguistic, etc.), Van Gennep arrives at the conclusion that none of them is sufficient in itself and that a variety of viewpoints is essential to one's interpretation, "while maintaining oneself within the specific atmosphere of folklore." This latter is difficult to define: "it is sensed and imagined much more than logically thought out and constructed" (p. 105). He nevertheless attempts to describe it by resorting to the concept of the philosopher Vaihinger, the "world-as-if" (die Welt als ob). The mechanisms of magic, folk medicine, astrology, and so on operate by means of extrapolations: on the basis of such and such a known fact one supposes certain consequences.

> The whole of folklore is bathed in the world-as-if. Most men...do not appear to be absolutely convinced of the existence of a God-Judge, or of direct intervention in

our personal affairs by Providence, or in some countries by local or universal divinities, or of the absolute truth of dogmas, or of the material reality of miracles. But they act as if they believed in them" (p. 106).

If the folklorist is thoroughly imbued with this concept, he will be working at the level of folk logic and feelings. And this is also the reason why the terms employed by folklore cannot be defined with any precision.

Having reached this point in his reflections, and contrary to all expectations, Van Gennep provides us with a definition of folklore: it is "the methodical study, in other words the science, of ways and customs" (p. 107). The term "popular" is omitted as valueless, since "ways and customs are general collective phenomena, discernible independently of race, type of civilization, social class, or, in certain countries (India), professional castes" (ibid.).

The definition is a brief one, but, even so, he goes back over it in order to make each term of it quite clear. Ways are ways of living; customs are ways of living that conform with "written or unwritten rules" to which people submit without external coercion. Ways are subject to an internal mechanism that remains always and everywhere the same and is dynamic not static. This mechanism has not yet been extensively studied; we see it in action, but we are not at all clear as to the exact process governing it.

Van Gennep also defines a number of other terms employed by folklorists. Belief ought not to be systematically opposed to science: belief also constitutes knowledge (see above, p. 86). Beliefs are expressed in actions that, in isolation, are observances or rituals. Combined into sequences, they become ceremonies. And "the systematized whole formed by ceremonies is the cult" (p. 109). This category of facts often presents a superficial aspect of incoherence, but this is reduced when one is able to establish the sequence of ideas and actions, which is often built up discontinuously, in stages. "These interruptions correspond to periods of rest in nature, to the halts one must take during a climb, to the sleep that provides rest from the activities of the day and enables one to recover one's depleted strength" (p. 110). This theory of stages—rites of passage—is thus based on a coincidence between social rhythms and natural rhythms. It makes possible the provision of a structural pattern that can be applied to a great number of folkloric data: magical and religious ceremonies, the organization of festivals and games, and family ceremonies "from cradle to grave." It is interesting to note that this theory, by which Van Gennep set such store, has become the de facto basis of his *Manuel*, or at least of that part he lived to complete. In the unfinished notes he made for his general conclusion to the work, he again employs the term "rhythm" and goes on to explain it: the system of classification adopted in the *Manuel*

> is rhythmic in the sense that it begins by considering
> the human life, the principal object of our interest, from
> its beginning to its end; then the cycle of the year; and
> lastly the manifestation of various activities divergent in
> direction yet all radiating from man as the center of
> energy. This rhythm, which is rectilinear in the first
> data series, then cyclic in the second, is alternating in
> the third. For here action is directed from subject to ob-
> ject, then rebounds from object back to subject.

In his introduction to the section entitled "Du Berceau à la tombe," Van Gennep contents himself with noting that these ritual stages play a considerable role in social life "because life itself progresses by oscillations and by stages" (p. 114). This idea, barely indicated in the *Manuel* as it stands or in *Les Rites de passage*, was presumably due to be developed further in the concluding section of the *Manuel*. In the event, it poses more questions than it solves. It would appear at first sight, for example, that this homology between natural rhythms and social rhythms is due to the fact that society models itself on nature, seeks in nature for the patterns on which to frame its own organization. Yet this interpretation would be difficult to reconcile with a great number of other statements to be found scattered throughout Van Gennep's works. For instance, in *Les Rites de passage* he stresses more than once that initiation ceremonies are celebrated on the occasion of social, not physical, puberty. Again, in an article that appeared in 1907 (*Religions, moeurs et légendes*, 1:189–201), dealing with the causal relations between physical environment and social, political, and economic organizations, he states: "One of the most interesting achievements of ethnography in recent years, and a paradoxical one at first sight, is the recognition that, far from modeling his social organization on nature, semicivilized man represents nature to himself as modeled on his own social organization" (p. 193). Van Gennep also opposes the astral interpretation of myths, reinstated by Ehrenreich and the Berlin school, because he was quite convinced in his own mind that it is the phases of men's own activities, not natural phenomena, that are the source material of such narratives. The problem could be formulated in terms of projection versus interiorization: do men project their social organization onto nature, or do they interiorize natural phenomena in their social organizations and representations? Van Gennep—it seems— preferred the first of these alternatives. He never investigated the underlying cause for that preference, but he would probably have subscribed to this passage from Lévi-Strauss criticizing a "naturalist" theory of myth: "there are no phenomena in the raw state: phenomena exist for man only when conceptualized and, as it were, filtered through logical and affective norms that form part of his culture."[3] It is along this line of thought, it would seem, that we ought to situate Van Gennep's theoretical position on this subject, even though he himself never really made it clear. It is at least a position that can be reconciled with the notion of a homology between life rhythms and social rhythms. For man is a living being and as such falls into the province of biology, as do his social organization and productions, since these are living phenomena. This homology between nature and culture is thus anchored at a very profound level. In this respect it is interesting to read an unpublished passage in which Van Gennep is dealing with the stylistic presentation of folkloric data:

> A folklorist, unless he is a pure theoretician and has never undertaken investigation in the field, is necessarily sensitive to lines (forms) and colors, to music and sounds, to others' psychic shifts and changing expression of them. What one might call professional contact with vital rhythms reacts on the rhythm of one's own writing; sympathy with the living is unconsciously expressed in the contouring of one's sentences and (transposed) sonorities that are often carried over from the local dialect into one's French.

We are not far here from unanimism, not to say pantheism.

Surveying the field of folklore as a whole, one does have the feeling that Van Gennep's concentration on ritual was accompanied by a corresponding neglect of folk beliefs. However, we must not forget that his first important work—*Tabou et totémisme à Madagascar*—was concerned with taboos, which are made up of both belief and ritual, mental representation and action (or suppressed action). It is the second aspect that interested him more, and particularly the third category of taboos (in his own classification): those whose underlying cause is to be found in a religious system, which is frequently totemic. The function of these particular taboos is in fact to strengthen the bonds between members of a single human and animal clan, between ancestors and descendants, between men and gods. They thus contribute to a very important social institution. However, though Van Gennep, in his study of rituals was well aware that their motive force was provided by the beliefs that underlay them, he was none too successful in isolating those beliefs as such in the case of European ethnography. For example, when dealing with the folk cult of Saint-Léonard (or Liénard), he observes that the name of the saint is directly connected with his function, which is to loosen (*délier*) bonds. Saint-Liénard is invoked to bring relief through release to prisoners, women in labor, and the sick. Van Gennep then goes on to suppose that the pun inherent in the saint's name may in fact be the source of the ritual, and he adds: "generally speaking, in theoretical studies of more or less civilized rituals there is too great a tendency to underestimate the importance of folk interpretations of a purely verbal order" (*Religion, moeurs et légendes*, 1:105). And belief does in fact fall into the verbal domain, yet we find once again that Van Gennep fails to exploit the field that his remarkable insight has opened up.

In the *Manuel*, he concentrates in the few lines he devotes to belief on the simple fact of belief as opposed to knowledge. He perceives two parallel and compatible psychic levels here; among the people these are seen to act concurrently, in much the same way that enabled great scientists like Pascal, Descartes, or Pasteur to reconcile science and faith in their lives and work. The place Van Gennep accords to beliefs in his work is in fact a reflection of the place they occupy in the material of folklore: they are not very conspicuous, and yet they are everywhere. If we read attentively the section dealing with the individual human life and seasonal ceremonies, we find beliefs surfacing everywhere, even though the overt subject matter is rituals. In the same way, direct observation never reveals belief as such; it is indeed very rare for an informant to begin a sentence with "people believe that. . . ." And yet, under the surface, the belief is always there, since it is the verbal element. Like speech, it cannot be seen, but it is there. In this sense Van Gennep's work is a faithful reflection of folklore's reality.

SEVEN

PROPERTY MARKS

There is a theme in Van Gennep's work, at once recurrent yet scattered, that might well escape attention if one confined oneself to reading his major works. Yet it is a theme that occupied a large place in his research, and its theoretical importance is far from negligible. I am referring to his study of property or ownership marks, brands, and armorial bearings.

This subject was in fact his first focus of interest in the ethnographic field, as is witnessed by an article published in 1901 in the *Revue des traditions populaires* (vol. 16, p. 403), entitled "Property Marks and Trademarks: Questionnaire for France, Switzerland, Italy, and Spain." We might note in passing that even at this early stage in his work he was employing the questionnaire method, thus reviving after a century the working method of the members of the Académie Celtique and the Société des Antiquaires. The replies he received provided him with material for a series of short articles printed in the same publication over a period of several years. In 1904 he announced (*Revue des*

Traditions populaires 19:273) a forthcoming book, to be called "Property Signs and Marks," that unhappily never materialized.[1] He then went on to state that his intention in the book would be to examine the relationships between alphabetiform marks and alphabets; he was in fact of the opinion that certain marks previously treated as merely whimsical are in fact vestiges of early alphabets. For instance, he had observed close resemblances, and sometimes even near identity, between Pyrenean property or ownership marks and certain siglas on Celtiberian coins. This incidental observation gives us a glimpse of the way in which, at the very outset of his research career, the focus of his interest moved from coins to property marks, in other words from a purely historical field to an ethnographic one.

Having moved on to a more specific study of Arab property marks, or *wasm*, Van Gennep arrived at the idea that the ancient Semitic alphabets were consciously formed, at various times and in various places, on the basis of these *wasm*. Broadening his field of inquiry, he then observed that the alphabetiform property marks, although identical in workmanship, are richer in form than the indigenous alphabets and that one finds property marks even among illiterate populations. One must therefore conclude that the alphabet derives from the marks and not vice versa. A further extension of property marks may be traced in the direction of heraldic signs, since the mark of a household, when placed on animals or things, also has the subsidiary purpose of signifying the filiation and social rank of the owner: "in all places where . . . society is subdivided into classes, the family (or household) property mark has taken on the signification of a coat-of-arms" ("Notes sur l'héraldisation des marques de propriété et les origines du blason," *Bulletin et mémoires de la Société d'anthropologie de Paris*,

5th ser. 6 [1905]: 103–12). Stated in these terms, the problem is an important one for ethnography, although Van Gennep in fact saw it as even wider than that, and in his *Titres et travaux scientifiques* of 1911 (pp. 15–16), he attempted to outline its scope:

> this study [the problem of property marks and signs] led me to put forward a personal explanation of certain prohibitions and even to revise the whole theory of taboo; to reconstruct the entire question of the origin of writing and alphabets on new foundations; to conduct research into the exact meaning of tattooing, body painting, and all mutilations implying the notion that such marks create a membership and kinship bond; to look into the value of current theories on the origins of armorial bearings; and to show that such bearings, and even the very language of heraldry, are older and more primitive than is ordinarily supposed; to examine, from this viewpoint, what the exact situation of specialized languages is in relation to languages in the usual sense, and so on. In short, this extended investigation into a subject as narrow at first glance as that of property marks and signs enabled me, indeed forced me, to review all the theories relating to prohibitions, systems of property-holding, and various forms of decorative art.

In reality Van Gennep was drawing up a work program there rather than a list of findings, since he had established the relationships he mentions in only a somewhat superficial way. A certain number of articles show that he was working on the problem, but in general they make rather disappointing reading when set against the comprehensive program sensed behind them and never completed. Answers to his questionnaire in the *Revue des traditions populaires* were probably somewhat sparse, but lack of documentation was never something that stopped Van

Gennep, and his polyglotism had enabled him to accumulate a considerable amount of material already. He had an intuition that it was in fact possible to construct a system from all these apparently disparate facts, but probably he was not vouchsafed the good luck, as he was with transition rituals, of finding their organizing principle, their "schema," and so was gradually forced to abandon the project. In 1938, in his bibliography for the *Manuel* (4:886) he notes that the material he had been accumulating for the past thirty years tended to confirm rather than weaken his theory that property marks should be seen as the origin of certain alphabets. In 1911 he mentioned the fact that his collection of property signs, brands, tattoos, and alphabetiform signs of all kinds already amounted to several thousand. In 1938 his unaided field investigations in Savoy alone had enabled him to collect a further 2,000.

In *Tabou et totémisme à Madagascar* (chap. 11, "Tabous de propriété" [Property Taboos]) he asserts that the property mark or sign was originally a taboo, for, "since ownership originally possessed a religious form, it is natural that the method of safeguarding property should likewise have a religious basis" (p. 183). And he had now discovered further proof of this in Madagascar, where the ownership mark branded onto cattle is in fact not at all distinctive and so cannot have any juridical value. The conclusion must be that sanction against theft is extranatural and that the brand is the sign of a taboo placed on the animal. Evidence had also been collected, among the Sakalaves, for the creation of a special language (the nomenclature of brands) and the attribution of a nobiliary value to property signs.

As far as totemism is concerned, we know that among certain Indian tribes of the Pacific Northwest the representation of the totem serves as both brand and kinship sign. But this relationship cannot be established everywhere and, specifically, not among the Australian aborigines.

Although Van Gennep gladly accepts the existence of a
connection between the two phenomena, he nevertheless
opposes Mauss's claim that the notions of god, totem pole,
name, and heraldic sign form an indissoluble unity in totemism (*Année sociologique* 8 [1905]: 242).
Having made a study of what he terms "special languages" (languages specific to a religion, to women, to
children, to a trade or profession, and so on), Van Gennep
then investigated the possible reasons for their existence,
and his conclusion was that

> they are merely one of the innumerable methods by
> which collectivities of every kind maintain their exist-
> ence and resist external pressures. For those who
> employ them, they are simultaneously a means of
> achieving cohesion and a protection against outsiders.
> ... Thus the special language plays the same role
> within the society as a whole that each general language
> plays in relation to other general languages. It is one of
> the consciously devised forms of differentiation that are
> necessary to the society's very existence (*Religions,
> moeurs et légendes*, 2:315–16).

Social life in fact oscillates constantly between two opposing and complementary tendencies: the tendency toward
cohesion and the tendency toward differentiation.
    These ideas are to be found again in another of Van
Gennep's books, one now wholly forgotten. This work,
entitled *Les Eléments extérieurs de la nationalité* and conceived
during the stressful years of the 1914–18 war and the subsequent Versailles Treaty negotiations, is the first volume
of his *Traité comparatif des nationalités*, the second and third
volumes of which, though planned, never in fact appeared. As its title indicates, the intention in this work was
to review all the external marks that nations employ for
the purpose of presenting themselves as such. "Every

organized group," Van Gennep writes, "in order to assert itself and maintain itself in existence, needs to distinguish itself from all other groups by visible marks, the study of which constitutes one of ethnography's most interesting branches" (p. 48). Body painting, tattoos, scarification, and mutilations constitute a primitive form of these signs of differentiation that enable an individual to be recognized as a member of his particular group. This primitive form was later replaced by the wearing of particular costumes. In Europe, for instance, the costumes worn by Slovaks, Magyars, and Serbs, to name only a few, have the value of a national symbol. Likewise, "the various rural costumes still found in Germany today can be seen to correspond to former territorial divisions, and are just one of the ways small groups have, in a country renowned for its local particularisms, of expressing their need and wish for differentiation" (p. 50). Up until the nineteenth century at least, in nations constituted for a great length of time (the majority of western European countries), costume provided an instant clue to the wearer's social class and also—from the Middle Ages onward—to his trade or profession. In such countries there occurred a transference of the feeling "expressed by the colors and cut of the clothes people wore . . . to colors and pieces of cloth displayed in a particular way": the standard, the flag. During the nineteenth century all states gradually adopted this means of differentiation. This was a deliberate and conscious process. Other signs of differentiation exist that are largely unconscious, such as the forms of individual dwellings and villages. These constitute an important element in social cohesion.

The most conspicuous and tenacious of these signs is language. History often shows that a group's loss of its language is accompanied by the loss of its social identity. As a result, a multiplicity of languages is an inherent characteristic of mankind. As early as 1908, in "Internationalisme et particularisme linguistique" (*Religions, moeurs et légendes*, 1:308–16), Van Gennep was asserting that universal languages, such as Esperanto or Volapük, are the product of utopian thought; even supposing that they could be imposed on the world, dialects would very soon arise that would eventually become just as impenetrable to one another as present-day Dutch, Spanish, and Greek. With reference to this differentiating role of language, he also puts forward a very subtle observation derived from his own personal experience: the fact that two groups speak languages closely akin to each other does not establish a feeling of community between them but, on the contrary, a feeling of opposition if not of actual hostility. "It seems that this linguistic kinship is seen by the groups involved as a threat to their specific individualities" (*Les Eléments extérieurs*, p. 80). Lévi-Strauss, in *La Pensée sauvage* (Paris: Plon, 1962), makes the same observation with reference to regional costumes in the peasant societies of eighteenth- and nineteenth-century Europe:

> That each community should have its own costume and that . . . it should be broadly made up of the same elements, was never even questioned: one simply did one's utmost to differentiate oneself from the next village, to outdo it in richness and inventiveness of detail. All women wore coifs, or caps, but these differed from district to district. . . . The double action of general conformism (which is the result of a closed universe) and parish particularism tends, here as elsewhere, among Australian aborigines as in our own peasant societies, to treat culture in accordance with the musical form of theme and variations (p. 119).

This feeling of opposition verging on hostility is also to be observed in what one might call folk heraldry, in other words the collective nicknames that neighboring villages bestow on each other.

The question of frontiers as an external sign of nationality brought Van Gennep back to his preoccupation with physical transition (see above, pp. 65 f.). All populations know the boundaries of their territory: primitive peoples know the precise extent of the area in which they may hunt, fish, and forage, and peasants know the borders of their fields. Methods of recognizing such boundaries make use of natural features such as stones, rocks, trees, water sources, and so on. Van Gennep intuitively understood this investment of the land by man. We have the proof of this in an article published in 1910, "Du sens d'orientation chez l'homme" (*Religions, moeurs et légendes* 3:33–61), in which he acknowledges that he himself possesses a well-developed sense of direction and attempts to fathom how it works:

> Upon analysis, I have always observed that this faculty for knowing where I am derives in the first place from a considerable accumulation of unconscious observations. My eyesight is excellent, and as I go along I automatically record the odd shape of a tree trunk, an oddly colored pebble, lengths of straw across the path (p. 35).

Then, in going on to analyze the confused sensation he experiences when he does lose his way, he concludes that it arises from a natural awareness of angles. His path is never straight, always a series of zigzags, and we know that determining an angle enables us to demarcate a fixed area of space. There is another way of appropriating territory, however, and that is to invest it with myth. In central Australia, for instance, the aborigines set great store by Beings who, in passing through a given territory, have accomplished remarkable feats, the memory of which is concretized in the form of natural features: springs, wells, isolated stones, rocks, hills, mountain chains, solitary trees, copses, and so on (*Mythes et légendes d'Australie*, p. cvii). This investment of a territory by means of myth is not confined to primitive peoples. European folklore teems with topographical beliefs and legends that literally map out the territories of various local groups.

The marks of territorial boundaries do not take the exclusive form of natural features. They may be invented by the social group and put in position intentionally, as in the case of the moat around early Rome, the great steles of the Assyrian kings, or the frontier posts of modern states. These marks possess a sacred character, "and to cross a boundary or frontier was, and still is for the more sensitive among us, like passing from one world into another. It was to perform a veritable magic and religious ritual" (*Les Eléments extérieurs*, p. 152). In short, it was a rite of pasasge. Moreover, the territorial boundary is not always a line. It can sometimes be a more or less broad expanse. The neutral zones around Greek cities served as market places and grazing land, and to enter them bearing arms was equivalent to a declaration of war. The marches of medieval times fall into this same category of intermediate zones, military no-man's-lands, buffer states, and so on.

An attentive perusal of this book, isolated though it is within Van Gennep's work as a whole, nevertheless enables us to perceive yet again the guiding threads that directed his research throughout his life: the notions of the rite of passage and of social, psychic, and physical thresholds, differentiation signs ensuring the social group's cohesion, appropriation of territory by means of myth and toponymy, the role played by the diversity of languages, and, lastly, his methodology itself, which

consists in "situating in series a certain number of phenomena hitherto viewed in isolation from one another,
discerning the internal bond between them, then isolating
the central mechanism by means of which that underlying
bond persists, despite variations of form, and gives the
whole series a particular aspect and power of survival"
(p. 47). In other words: the comparative method.

EIGHT

FOLKLORE AND HISTORY

We have remarked in passing on Van Gennep's attitude with regard to history and have noted that it was an attitude not without ambiguity. It would therefore be no bad thing to review the development of his views on this question stage by stage.

The 1908 article entitled "La Valeur historique du folklore" (*Religions, moeurs et légendes* 2:173–85) belongs to the period when Van Gennep regarded history as a discipline that enables one merely to describe facts, whereas the ethnographic (or comparative) method explains them (see "Tabou, totémisme et méthode comparative," ibid., 2:22–88). Not only that, but ethnography could also be an invaluable aid to history, since ethnographical material can possess historical value if one knows how to apply the necessary correctives to it. For instance, in folk literature it is essential to differentiate the "cultural layers" involved, in other words the successive additions made over the centuries. In *Mythes et légendes d'Australie* Van Gennep had established a very useful criterion in this respect: it appears that the survival of memories relating, not to beliefs or customs, but to raw facts is normally of the order of a century to a century and a half, in other words the duration of five to six generations. This criterion is obviously valid only for populations without writing. It will be remembered that later, in his *L'Etat actuel du problème totémique*, Van Gennep most emphatically reversed his position on this point:

> It is now beyond doubt that these myths and legends have as little scientific and documentary value from the social point of view as from the ethnic, zoological, or botanical point of view. I would consequently ask my readers to consider null and void any arguments I may have based in previous publications on the idea that we ought to accept as genuine historical evidence the passages in myths and legends concerning the former social state of the aborigines (p. 140).

This reversal of opinion is an important milestone in his work, since it enabled him to establish the exact nature of mythical evidence; he now saw myth, at least as far as the aborigines are concerned, as the receptacle for the social group's yearning for an idyllic state of existence, a state it had projected backward to a prehistoric time, a Golden Age or paradise. To take that desire for a reality would be to commit the same error as that made by medieval theologians when they took Genesis literally as an explanation of the formation of the world, the differentiation of the species, and the necessity to work. This change in his way of thinking doubtless seems to us the most elementary of steps, a necessary preliminary without which ethnography could not even exist. Yet it is one that must be taken by anyone who wishes to engage in that discipline (if not in any "science of man"). In those days this question was perhaps not as clear as it is to us, and the idea of survivals, for instance, so dear to the British school, still provided cover for a great deal of equivocation.

Van Gennep gradually widened this rift he had opened between history and ethnography. The essential distinction between them, as he saw it, derives from the fact that history studies dead evidence while ethnography deals with living evidence. The superiority of the latter is thus dazzlingly apparent: it can allow itself to view past facts as living by placing them back into their former present and by taking into account all the appropriate factors that would have operated at that time. This is the gist of what Van Gennep asserts in his *Titres et travaux* of 1911, where his tone becomes almost prophetic when he writes:

> I became convinced very rapidly that if the nineteenth century was the century of historical science, then the twentieth was to be that of the ethnographical sciences and that, just as the last century enabled us to conceive mankind in depth, by the diffusion of a perspectived conception that is nowadays called the *historical sense*, so our own century will provide a conception of much greater breadth, derived from the detailed and systematic observation of living evidence, a conception that one may term the *ethnographic sense*. . . . And if I were not a little apprehensive of being reproached with exaggeration, I would say that ethnography in the twentieth century will prove the foundation upon which a new philosophic conception of mankind will be constructed (p. 21).

The essential criticism to be made of history is that it can never do anything but juxtapose, whereas ethnography combines. And it follows from this that the first can never actually explain anything. It studies forms only, whereas ethnography not only deals with factors and mechanisms but actually studies them in action. In *Le Folklore* his tone becomes rather more acrimonious; here the historical point of view has become a "psychic and methodological malady" from which we must free ourselves by means of a "psychic displacement" that will enable us to adopt the biological method (pp. 32–35). Varagnac, in his book *Civilisations traditionelles et genres de vie* ([Paris: Albin Michel, 1948], p. 59) described this position of Van Gennep's as "doctrinaire" and his conception of folklore as a "fundamental countertruth." He claims in fact that folk traditions are by now dead and that their decline began after the 1870 war. The only method capable of studying them is, consequently, the historical method.

Pushed to their extremes, these opposing viewpoints are in fact equally untenable. Although it is true that the early twentieth century did see a very marked decline in traditions, it is also true that more of them have remained viable than is generally believed and that new ones are still being created (Van Gennep's "nascent facts"). On the other hand, the claim that folklore can dispense with history entirely will not bear scrutiny. In fact, Van Gennep himself surreptitiously reintroduces history when, in the same work, he speaks of the "chain of tradition" into which facts observed in the present must be inserted (see above, p. 73). In the *Manuel*, he expresses the opinion that the polemic between the historical and ethnographic is outdated in view of the incontestable victory of the latter. And yet he is obliged occasionally to speculate as to the date of origin of certain customs. For instance, when dealing with family ceremonies "from cradle to grave" he notes the large number of folklore intrusions into the Christian ritual, and he thinks that these are autonomous inventions dating for the most part from the early Middle Ages. Any attempt to make them into pagan survivals would necessitate putting forward a hypothesis for which there are no possible proofs. Such proofs cannot be found in any resemblances that might be observed with the customs and beliefs of so-called primitive civilizations, "since the possibilities for invention and modification in the psychic and ceremonial domain that constitutes folklore are not unlimited in number" (*Manuel*, p. 824).

Thirty-eight years earlier he was expressing himself in much the same way with reference to the legends of saints:

> In fact our Middle Ages were a period of collective creation on the basis of a fund of original material created at that moment almost from scratch, material in which older elements are present as indisputable survivals only in small quantities. . . . The identity of customs and beliefs can frequently be explained very simply indeed, and without resort to the notion of survivals, by the identity of the theoretical guiding principles underlying them: sympathy, antipathy, transmissibility of qualities by contact or over distances, trajectory of magico-religious forces, condensation, diffusion, and conservation of energy (*Religion, moeurs et légendes*, 1:115).[1]

Though he is unwilling to admit it, Van Gennep is unable to eliminate history totally from folklore research. When one attempts to pin down exactly what it was he had against the historical method, one very soon becomes convinced that his antagonism derives essentially from a misunderstanding. Clearly it was necessary, in the first quarter of the twentieth century, to provide the as yet incompletely constituted science of ethnography with an independent status and to free it, in particular, from the domination of history. Seen in this light, Van Gennep's mode of expression is doubtless in part the product of a legitimate pride in his subject:

> We are claiming autonomy for our science; we think that it has made sufficient progress during the past hundred years to have earned the right to reject the

leading-strings of childhood and to take its rightful
place—still young, no doubt, but adolescent at last—
beside its elders, history, archeology, and geography,
which were once its godmothers—and somewhat jeal-
ous godmothers, it is true. The former relationship of
subordination can now be transformed into one of
mutual aid and equality (*Titres et travaux*, p. 4).

It is also interesting to note that Van Gennep is in agreement on this point with Durkheim, even though the latter's feelings on the matter were not quite so intense. As
Lévi-Strauss has shown, Durkheim's attitude toward history underwent a clearly perceptible change between 1892
and 1912.[2] The credit he gradually withdrew from history
in that period he invested in ethnography. Whereas he saw
the data of ethnography in 1892 as no more than a com-
plement to historical evidence and requiring confirmation
by the latter, by 1912, in *Les Formes élémentaires de la vie
religieuse*, it was from the former that he believed the coming renovation of the study of human societies was to derive.

The misunderstanding turns in fact on differing concep-
tions of history. When Van Gennep speaks in *Le Folklore* of
placing ethnographic observations made in the present
within a series he terms the "chain of tradition," he is
saying that one must study the antecedents of such evidence. Is that still ethnography, or is it already history?
The reverse also occurs, and he foresaw that "every historian who wishes to understand the reasons for the existence of ancient institutions finds himself obliged, sooner
or later, to break through the barriers erected by tradition
and address himself to ethnographic evidence" (*Religions,
moeurs et légendes*, 1:230). He consequently has high praise
for Edouard Meyer, the first part of whose *Histoire de l'an-
tiquité* is wholly devoted to ethnography. In the *Manuel*

(1:96, no. 5) he also applauds the attempt made by Marc
Bloch to "tackle history backwards," in other words to explain past events by present-day facts—the past by the
present and not vice versa, as the historical tradition had
demanded until then.

In an article entitled "La Tombe d'Alaric" (*Revue ar-
chéologique* 19 [1924]: 195–207) he gives a very good example
of this method. He begins by demonstrating the disarray of
historians when confronted by chronicles interspersed
with more or less legendary interpolations that they are
unable to disentangle from the historical facts. We know
that Alaric, king of the Goths, died in southern Italy in 410.
For his burial, the course of the Busento River was
diverted, a deep ditch was dug in the exposed riverbed,
the king was buried in it with a great quantity of treasure,
the river was restored to its normal course, and the slaves
who had dug the grave were sacrificed so that no one
would know the spot where the treasure lay buried. How
much in this chronicle is historical fact, and how much is
legend? The historians, unable to answer that question,
were tempted, out of scientific scruple, to classify the
entire story as legend. Van Gennep, on the other hand,
using the ethnographic method, was able to solve the problem. He searched for other examples of this mode of burial
among the material accumulated by other ethnographers.
They were few but consistent. He found in fact only six
accounts of what he proposed calling "subaquatic burial."
In every case this form of burial was employed solely for
individuals of a certain class, that is to say great leaders,
supreme chiefs. And all six examples contained the same
elements: diversion of a river, digging of a vast grave,
deposit of treasure, and subsequent sacrifice, sometimes of
the chief's wives as well, but in every case of the slaves
who took part in the work. The justification for this last

practice is the same as in Alaric's case: left alive, the slaves
might be tempted to return and dig up the buried wealth.
For Van Gennep this last feature is legendary and to be
classed with innumerable other folktales concerning buried
treasure. In reality, what this form of interment was intended to protect was not so much the treasure as the
remains of the leader himself. Had his bones been scattered, he could not have continued to protect his people
and his land, to go on reigning after death. According to
the chronicle, it was Alaric himself who had expressed the
wish to be interred in this way, in order to perpetuate his
right to the possession of Italy. And Van Gennep adds:
"To bury a chief is like burying coals, coins, or a boundary
stone: it is a ritual of appropriation. In the case of a chief,
his ownership of the territory is being established on behalf
of his subjects and fellow citizens, the still living who occupy its surface." It is therefore indispensable that his burial place should remain absolutely inviolate.

What Van Gennep wanted in fact—whether consciously
or unconsciously—was the kind of history we are actually
seeing emerge today, derived, as it happens, from the
work of Marc Bloch, the historian Van Gennep admired. It
is a history in which interdisciplinary border disputes have
been eliminated, in which the various methodologies com-
plement rather than exclude or compete with one another.
It is this development that Jacques Le Goff expressed so
well in the article—exemplary with regard to the question
concerning us here—written in collaboration with Leroy-
Ladurie and entitled "Mélusine maternelle et défricheuse":

> Thus structuralism and comparative history, if they
> help to eliminate a fallacious historicism, that of the
> "factual" historicity of folktales and legends (which
> entails seeking the explanation and, worse still, the

source of a tale or legend in a historical event or personage), also enable us, if we pay attention not only to
the form but to its shifting content, to achieve a much
better grasp of their historical function in relation to social and ideological structures themselves (*Annales*,
May-August 1971, pp. 587–622).

NINE

CONCLUSION

This book is appearing in the year when Van Gennep would have reached his hundredth birthday. Yet his work still displays all the attributes of youth, and we have still not explored all its riches or all the instruction it contains.

His greatest merit was probably that of having constituted French folklore as such. Not that France had not previously benefited from the labors of a great many folklorists of value. Dergny, Sébillot, and Saintyves spring immediately to mind, and we must not forget the legion of obscure local savants, the multitude of provincial learned societies, who continued their assiduous accumulation of evidence, year after year, throughout the nineteenth century and the early part of the twentieth. But all that, because of the disparate nature of the material and the total—or almost total—lack of method involved, did not yet constitute a true whole. Van Gennep performed a vast labor of synthesis, first by extending his own investigations to a number of regions scarcely studied before (in 1937 alone he drew more than 2,000 parishes into his net) and second by collecting together most of the available earlier documents in his *Manuel*. We have seen that he was not able to complete that work and that a certain number of topics are still missing from it. Even these, however, do appear in the bibliography, which, despite the fact that it has not been republished since his death, remains an unrivaled working tool. The *Manuel* therefore constitutes a synthesis of France's entire folkloric past. It is also a methodological tool for use in future research. Van Gennep had perfected a questionnaire, the one first used in Savoy, that can in fact be modified as circumstances and the particular region under examination require. In their preface to volume 1, part 7, of the *Manuel*, devoted to the Twelve Days of Christmas cycle, which appeared after the author's death, Lecotté and Rivière testify both to the efficacy of his methodology and to his concern for synthesis:

> The nearer publication of the *Manuel* drew, the more the existing documentation was shown to be deficient. On many occasions we ourselves witnessed the Master being obliged to instigate, and even to carry out in person, some particular and indispensable study project required to cover some unexplored topic. How many questionnaires he must have sent out at the eleventh hour, across the length and breadth of France, in order to collect the details he needed to structure the whole and to establish the essential characteristics of a chapter (pp. x–xi).

Yet, although he was only too familiar with the merits of his own questionnaires, having put them so often to the test, Van Gennep was also able to perceive value in those devised by others, since he published a number of them as the first item in his bibliographical volumes. This bibliography as a whole therefore constitutes a remarkable research tool.

We have seen that Van Gennep's concept of the rite of passage, or transition ritual, provided a heuristic schema of great importance for folklore, since it made it possible to organize the subject's heterogeneous and tangled mass of material. His sequence method, which was closely akin to the rites-of-passage concept, then provided the true methodological foundation of modern folklore studies while, at the same time, demonstrating the futility of earlier comparative work, which had assembled its data merely by drawing parallels between superficially shared characteristics. In other words, the Frazerian method was rendered obsolete (though that does not mean that Frazer's work has lost its interest, which is to be sought elsewhere). For Van Gennep, in fact, rituals and social acts in general had no intrinsic or constant meaning or value. Their meaning and their value depend on the whole of which they form a part and, more particularly, on the rituals and acts that precede and follow them.

> Hence we conclude that in order to understand a ritual, an institution, or a technique, it must not be arbitrarily extracted from the ceremonial, juridical, or technological whole of which it forms a part. On the contrary, one must always consider each element of that whole in its relation with all the other elements (*Titres et travaux*, p. 24).

Here I should like to refer back to the example Van Gennep himself gives of this method: the aspersion ritual that is part of the marriage ceremony in Savoy (see above, p. 67). There he shows very clearly how the identical ritual takes on different meanings according to the various ceremonial and cultural contexts in which it is performed. We can thus describe him as a comparativist, as we do Frazer, but we can then go on to say that, unlike Frazer, he compares superficially similar facts in order to show that they often, if not always, have different meanings. This sequence method derives from the concept of the transition ritual, but it completes that concept during the data-treatment stage. The former makes possible a formal organization of the tangled mass of facts; the latter enables one to penetrate to their meaning by taking account of their place within the formal whole previously established.

This double contribution of Van Gennep's to the theory of folklore is fundamental, but it is not his only one. We can find in his work a number of ideas, methods, and research techniques that are part of the common currency of folklore research today, even though folklorists themselves do not always give their inventor credit for them.

Of these contributions it is probably Van Gennep's cartographical method that is best known. He gives an account of its practical aspect in the introduction to his *Manuel de folklore français contemporain* (pp. 85–95) and of the theory behind it in an article, published in 1934 in the Italian review *Lares*, entitled "Contribution à la méthodologie du folklore." This method consists in indicating on a map of the region under scrutiny, parish by parish, the presence or absence of a particular cultural feature (ritual, belief, cult, and so on). There are several observations that must be made here. First, Van Gennep's method was inherently opposed to what he termed the "sampling method" that a great number of folklore workers, such as Sauvé, Rocal, Cosquin, and others, used in their monographs. And indeed, if one reads their works attentively, one soon becomes aware that their investigations have been carried out, not throughout a region or entire province, as the titles of their books might lead one to believe, but only in a small number of parishes or perhaps only a single one. Such samplings, Van Gennep says, no doubt have their value in exploring for oil or in chemical analysis, but they have none whatever in folklore research. The criticism he makes of Sébillot is different and concerns the fact that Sébillot called his work *Folklore de France*. In reality, what Sébillot does is to present facts, collected in the various French provinces, without giving the slightest indication of whether these facts are widespread or rare, normal or aberrant. The cartological method, in contrast, constrains the researcher to a certain honesty, both because it reveals the limits of his investigation and because its value is a function of the investigation's degree of exhaustiveness.

What results can we expect from the making of these maps? We must not attribute any absolute explanatory value to them, Van Gennep tells us. Their principal function is to reveal folkloric zones. These in turn help us toward a comprehension of the data themselves—their nature, their origin, and their diffusion. For instance, after completing his investigations in Savoy and duly indicating the incidence of a number of features on his map of the region, Van Gennep was able to establish with certainty that the folkloric phenomena concerned displayed a number of somewhat unexpected characteristics. First, he perceived that these phenomena had evolved on a plane completely independent of the natural or geographical plane; mountains, deserts, rivers, and plains had clearly neither impeded their diffusion nor yet favored it. Then he tried to establish whether the folkloric zones revealed on his maps coincided with the boundaries of dioceses, which we know to have been extremely stable in France from the end of the Roman Empire onward, since the Roman administrative districts did not change their boundaries when they became religious dioceses or nonreligious mandates. Again no coincidence was apparent. We then have to ask what the positive criteria actually are that govern the appearance and diffusion of folklore-related phenomena. In the case of saint cults in Savoy, Van Gennep was able to establish these with some precision. He could see, as we have said, that a given saint cult, liturgical as well as popular, could straddle the boundary between two dioceses, taking root in this place or that quite independently of any central authority. The propagation factors, when ascertained, turned out to have been ecclesiastical figures (bishops), members of the nobility (their changes of residence dictated by the play of matrimonial alliances), or, in many cases, convents, guilds, or endowed institutions. This means that at least some of the factors involved could be equated with individual actions, a fact that provides support for the thesis, already strengthened by Van Gennep's other field investigations, that the popular or folk can never be equated with the collective; the sources and transformations of folklore material are to be sought in individuals and not in the folk as a whole, which in fact constitutes simply the medium of propagation and transmission (see above, pp. 72 and 92).

In his "Contribution à la méthodologie du folklore," Van Gennep deals with all the problems to which the existence of folklore zones gives rise, including, apart from those just mentioned, the problem that might be called negative incidence. It would of course be easy to assert that any data absent from a particular zone have quite simply disappeared. But in that case it would be desirable first to provide textual evidence showing that they previously existed and then to explain exactly why they have disappeared—both in a general way and why in certain localities and not in others; why the disappearances are topographically grouped rather than random and isolated; and why, finally, they survived in the positive zones. Van Gennep takes the example of the charivari (a general village festivity on the occasion of remarriage by a widow or widower).

This custom was officially forbidden by both religious and
civil authorities in Savoy at least as early as the fifteenth
century, and there were fixed penalties for ignoring the
prohibitions. Normally the custom ought to have lapsed,
yet it was clear that nothing of the sort had happened. The
custom appeared almost everywhere as positive; if occasionally it was marked in as absent, that was because there
was no longer any opportunity to celebrate it, since remarriage of widowed persons was very rare. "Thus these
negative findings are not absolute; they signify merely that
the custom is *latent*. And I am fairly sure that this precise
indication of *latent customs* is likewise one of the new
results of my investigation and presentation" ("Contribution à la méthodologie du folklore," p. 31).

This method does in fact employ a genuine positive-
negative dialectic, a point on which Van Gennep dwells
both repeatedly and emphatically, employing that particular tone of conviction always apparent when he is absolutely certain of the truth of his intuitions (as in the case of
his rite-of-passage concept; see p. 58). The originality of his
cartographic method lies in this indication of negative as
well as positive features:

> I have improved . . . this method, in the field of French
> folklore, by supplementing the positive element, which
> has alone been taken into account hitherto, with the
> negative element, which to my way of thinking also has
> a positive value from the point of view of interpreta-
> tion, albeit on the far side of zero. I would also add
> that, when I employ the term zero, the value I attribute
> to it is likewise variable, since all psychic and social
> values are complex, and making our zero a fixed point
> must always be an arbitrary operation (pp. 24–25).

We have just seen how absence can conceal presence:
present absence but former presence; apparent absence but
latent presence. But even beyond this, all of it still within

the domain of historical contingency, there is yet another factor, one that Van Gennep himself fails to make wholly explicit: the negative is just as much a constituent of existence as the positive. A folklore zone is defined equally by the features that are found within it and by those that are not but that may be present in a neighboring zone. That is indeed how a zone is constituted. It is in this context that Van Gennep recalls how, as early as 1904, in his book *Tabou et totémisme à Madagascar* he asserted that the taboo —in other words, a form of prohibition—was equivalent to a positive ritual and not to be regarded as an institution apart. The expression of the taboo is negative, of course, but its function is wholly positive.

In the introduction to his *Manuel* Van Gennep returns to the merits and limitations of his cartographical method. The maps can reveal coincidences in the distribution of various cultural features. But, as is shown by the examples he gives, it is the absence of coincidence that is revealed most clearly:

> Thus one discovers, for example, that the feudal land-holding system had no effect on the people's language or ways. We also see . . . that the divisions into provinces and departments do not correspond to the divisions into folklore zones; or again, if we take the various categories of folklore, we see that there is no geographical coincidence between them, so that the territorial incidence of marriage-ceremony features, for example, is quite different from the incidence of saint cults or local feast days (pp. 104–5).

In other words, the maps as such provide no interpretation; they merely pose the problems for us on the concrete basis of the facts themselves.

It is on the level of psychic constituents that interpretation must be sought. It is striking fact that Van Gennep, throughout his work, consistently resorts to psychology when he reaches the final stage of his analysis, for instance in *La Formation des légendes*, back in 1910, after he has shown how the transformations of mythic motifs come about (see above, p. 46) or again, in the *Manuel*, when he compares the world of folklore to Vaihinger's "the world as if" (see p. 96). He does the same, too, in "Contribution à la méthodologie du folklore," where he asserts that the aim of a folklore monograph is

> to show the interaction of the feelings, concepts, and judgments that constitute individual psychic activity and collective psychic activity within a given social group . . . since the ultimate problem is always that of evaluating the often ephemeral relations between constants and variants (pp. 28–29).

From the fragmentary and still unpublished notes he made for his conclusion to the *Manuel* it is evident that he had planned to develop his ideas on folklore zones at some length, in particular those concerning the question of the territorial units constituted by the *pagi* or *pays* in French folklore. Here again he asserted that the resemblances and differences among these "units" cannot be explained by geology, by human or economic geography, by political or administrative history, or by linguistics, and he concludes:

> If this is accepted, then the notion of the *pays* falls much more into the realm of psychology than into that of any other discipline and appears as partially subordinated to a community of language (more precisely, of sub-dialect), to a community of moral and mental orienta-tion, and to a community of interests.

It is difficult in 1973 to gauge the extent of Van Gennep's contributions to the methodology of folklore simply because they have by now become its undisputed founda-tions. He brought the era of the amateur in his field to a close. By this I do not mean to imply that the work of such amateurs was without interest—far from it, for it is sometimes far greater than more recent studies by "clever dabblers" (as Van Gennep would have called them) who think all they have to do is abandon the henceforth despised term "folklore" in order to render their researches scientific. Van Gennep, by contrast, employed all his considerable rigor and intellectual honesty in the cause of rehabilitating folklore studies. By rejecting the sampling method, he made clear the necessity for conducting inquiries in every parish of the region under investigation. Not only did his cartographic method provide the proof of this, it also made possible a presentation of the material collected while, at the same time, revealing latent problems and hypotheses by defining the boundaries of folklore zones.

From the theoretical point of view he shed light on the dialectic inherent in the data of folklore by means of antitheses such as absence/presence, constants/variants, individual/collective, latent/actual, positive/negative, and so on. As early as 1909 he proclaimed the absolute necessity of not isolating customs, rituals, beliefs, or mythical themes from their contexts if we are not to let their meaning elude us. He stresses this point yet again in his unpublished notes: "A custom is the expression of a psychic, rational, emotional, and social complex; moreover, a custom does not exist on its own: it is linked organically with all the others."

Despite its jumbled and somewhat chaotic surface appearance, his work as a whole is remarkably coherent, yet without ever giving the impression of rigidity or dogmatism; reflexive and methodological schemas are to be found (we have just seen one more example) in his earliest published works as well as in his last (and even in his notes for books still in the project stage). Yet I have had occasion to remark on several occasions that Van Gennep was a poor theoretician. And it is true that he had difficulty in systematizing the concepts and ideas he discovered; he produced schemas enabling him to organize them, but he never developed them into a genuine theory. In a somewhat paradoxical fashion, that is perhaps Van Gennep's greatest merit and the essential interest of his work. This absence of theory leaves his reader at total liberty, without detracting in any way from the value of the facts presented. Quite the contrary in fact. We may say, therefore, that Van Gennep was guided by what is commonly called intuition, and that was a quality he certainly did not lack. But intuition is in reality nothing more than the ability of the unconscious to function freely during the process of selecting and organizing facts. Theoreticians inhibit its freedom of action by interposing their theoretical edifices, abstract constructions that oblige them to screen their facts in such a way as to risk introducing a bias into them. The work of authors like Van Gennep, on the other hand (and, in a slightly different sense, like Frazer) is far more useful as material for later interpretations. One has the certainty that their documents have the authenticity of the unconscious, since their work has been carried out, in a way, from unconscious to unconscious, from a so-called "collective" unconscious to an individual unconscious. And whereas the work of the theoreticians ossifies, as the years pass, and is drained of all interest in the end, except for the historian of ideas, the work of someone like Van Gennep can ride with the tide of science's own development, since it remains constantly fresh, living, protean, and mobile.

We have seen from the many quotations from his books and articles how clear and comprehensible his way of expressing himself always remained and how his style, without being of any great beauty, was never without its charm. "I was lucky," he writes in his article "Contribution à la méthodologie du folklore," "in regarding myself as a son of the French eighteenth century, not of the nineteenth. In other words, I had the supreme good fortune to be apprehensive of concealing my thought beneath so-called technical terms. . . . Psychologists of any value have always managed to describe even their subtler shades of meaning in simple words" (p. 28). He always observed the principle that "the more complex a problem is, the more reason to find a way of presenting it simply. That was the opinion of Montaigne, of Descartes, and of our whole heritage of thinkers . . . without any specialized vocabulary" (ibid.). As for the charm of his style, it is the charm of his personality itself: forthright, sincere, authentic, generous, comprehensive, full of humanity, and yet not lacking in either dignity or rigor.

APPENDIX

EXCERPTS FROM VAN GENNEP'S WRITINGS

What Is Ethnography?

The proper domain of ethnography is the time of beginnings: it makes a direct study of the factors and modalities of the very *genesis* of human activities; it seeks to discern the exact starting point of man's arts, techniques, institutions, ways of feeling and thinking, speaking and singing, drawing and crafting; and it is ethnography that thus lays down the foundations upon which, thanks to all the other branches of study, a precise and complete knowledge of man as doer and thinker can be built up.

To the list of limitations given earlier we can now add the following: ethnography is not the general science of civilizations; it is rather, if I may so express it, the *introduction to the general science of civilizations*. It analyzes cultural phenomena in their relatively primitive forms. And I stress that word *relatively*, for it would not cross anyone's mind that it is still possible in our day, in any place on earth, to come across evidence of an absolutely primitive civilization. On the other hand, the progress of natural and histor-

ical knowledge has made it impossible to accept so
localized and so rare a phenomenon as degeneration as a
generality. Although now outdated, this theory of the degeneration of human societies, or their "depravation," as
they said in the eighteenth century, still attracts a few be-
lated adherents, who believe, as though in some article of
faith, that man in his beginnings was perfect and possessed of all truth. It is certain that this opinion remains
beyond all means of verification and also outside any scientific discussion. It is not our task to reconstruct a hypotheti-
cal primitive man but to strive, through a close and totally
unbiased examination of what men are today, to understand what men may have been in earlier times.

For me, man is in nature, not outside nature or above it;
he is therefore subject to the great natural laws of con-
stancy, variability, and fluctuation. These laws may be discerned as much in the evolution of civilizations as in that of
living beings; and ethnography as I see it has no right to
ignore the fact that one of its most important objects must
therefore be to determine in what forms these great general
laws govern human activities. That is why, as an introduc-
tory science, it must lay the foundations of what one might
call the philosophy of techniques, just as it provides an
introduction to the philosophy of art, language, and the
mind. I am well aware that the term "philosophy" used in
this sense is old-fashioned, but it does at least have the
merit of enabling me to express more succinctly the following: that ethnography is not merely descriptive, that it has
a duty to cooperate in the solution of the great problems
posed by the application of the idea of evolution to mental
and cultural phenomena. While being a pure science and a
science of direct research, ethnography must therefore also
contribute its share—and it is not a small share—to the
construction of general syntheses.

                    (*Titres et travaux*, pp. 16–17)

The Comparative Method

This principle is very simple. When earlier "com-
parativists," if I may call them that, wished to study a
phenomenon, they used to accumulate parallels taken
from all sorts of civilizations and all sorts of ceremonial
wholes, not worrying in the slightest about any concomitant conditions, with the aim of showing that no known
phenomenon, however strange or bizarre it might appear,
is singular or meaningless.

But the striking thing is this: that the meaning found by
this method, in a ritual or a technique viewed in isolation,
is never other than a superficial meaning. It was in vain
that Tuchmann went on, year after year, collecting all the
documents he could lay his hands on relating to witchcraft,
for he came not a single step nearer to solving the question
that arises every time one comes to study an example of
witchcraft in a specific set of local, ethnic, and cultural
conditions. I therefore attempted to establish what the
boundaries are within which ethnographical comparison is
permissible and reliable by examining first rituals, then
myths, legends, and folktales, and, last of all, techniques.

The result of my inquiry, which took me a dozen or so
years, is that no ritual or social act possesses a value or an
intrinsic meaning capable of a once-and-for-all definition.
Each will change its value and its meaning according to the
actions that precede and follow it. The conclusion that
must therefore be drawn is that, in order to understand a
ritual, an institution, or a technique, we must not extract it
arbitrarily from the ceremonial, juridical, or technological
whole of which it forms a part; we must always, on the
contrary, consider each element of that whole in its relations with all the other elements. The term "sequence
method" expresses precisely the specific characteristic of
this attitude: in order for ethnographic comparison to ac-

quire its true value, what we must compare are sequences
or series of facts, not isolated facts. And that was the end of
one of the great arguments of the purely historical school
against our method.

(*Titres et travaux*, pp. 23–24)

Rites of Passage

We have now come to the end of our brief review of the
ceremonial cycles through which man passes in all the
serious circumstances of his life. It has been barely even a
sketch of a vast fresco whose every detail should by rights
be studied with care.

We have seen the individual categorized into various
compartments, synchronically or successively, and obliged
from the day of his birth to that of his death, in order to
pass from one of those compartments to another, or in
order to be able to join a group made up of other individuals categorized into other compartments, to submit to
ceremonies that may often be diverse in their forms but are
always alike in their mechanisms. Sometimes the individual was alone in his confrontation with all these groups;
sometimes he was a member of a group separated from
groups formed by others. The two broad primary divisions
were based either on sex—men on one side, women on the
other—or on magico-religious considerations—the profane
on one side, the sacred on the other. These two divisions
cut through all societies, from one end of the world to the
other and throughout history. Then there are the specialized groupings formed by divisions that occur in some
general societies only: religious societies, totemic groups,
phratries, castes, professional classes. Within each society
we then also find age sets, the family, and politico-

administrative and geographic units (province, parish). Alongside this complex world of the living there are also the worlds inhabited before birth and after death. All these are the constants, to which we then added various particular and temporary events: pregnancy, illnesses, dangers, journeys, and so on. And always and everywhere an identical aim conditioned an identical form of activity. For groups as for individuals, to live is to be split up and be reconstituted without cease, to change both state and form, to die and be reborn. It is to act, then to stop, to wait and rest, only to begin acting again, but differently. And always there are fresh thresholds to be crossed, the thresholds of summer or winter, of season or year, of month or falling night; the threshold of birth, of adolescence, of maturity; the threshold of old age; the threshold of death; and the threshold of the other life—for those that believe in it.

(*Les Rites de passage*, pp. 271–72)

Physical Transition

Although as a general rule the territory occupied by a semicivilized tribe is defined only by natural features, its inhabitants and their neighbors know perfectly well where the territorial boundaries of their rights and prerogatives lie. The natural frontier may be marked by a rock or a tree, a sacred river or lake, which it is forbidden to cross or pass beyond, under pain of supernatural punishment. But this case does seem to be somewhat rare. Often the boundary is indicated by an object—a post, a gateway, or an upright stone (milestone, boundary stone, and so on) that has been put in position to the accompaniment of consecrating rites. The protection afforded by the prohibition may be direct or indirect (intervention of frontier divinities, for example, those represented on Babylonian kudurrus, or Hermes, Priapus, and other boundary-stone divinities). By the ceremonial installation of boundary stones or physical demarcation lines (plowed furrow, strips of animal hide, ditch, and so on), a fixed area of land is appropriated by a specific grouping in such a way that to enter that reserved space, if one is an outsider, is to commit sacrilege in just the same way as the profane person does when he enters a sacred grove, a temple, and so on. . . .

The ban on entering such a territory thus has the character of a supernaturally sanctioned prohibition, which is expressed by means of boundary stones, walls, and statues in the classical world and by means of simpler methods among the semicivilized. It goes without saying that these signs are not positioned along the entire boundary line, any more than our modern frontier posts are, but only at crossing points, on roads, and at crossroads. The simplest method consists in placing some sign in the middle of the path or across it, such as a bundle of herbs, a length of wood, a sheaf of some cereal crop attached to a stake, and so on. Already more complicated is the erection of a gateway, which may or may not be decorated with natural objects or statues of varying degrees of refinement. In short, there is a whole variety of procedures, which I need not describe in detail here.

(*Les Rites de passage*, pp. 20–22)

"Lives of the Saints" and Newspaper Serials

Having recently read and compared a number of *Lives of the Saints*, I have been left with the impression that such *Lives* and *Passions*, recounting the stories of saints and martyrs, were, quite simply, the only possible medieval equivalent of our own newspaper serials of today.

We find the same constant changes of fortune; the same suspensions of dramatic interest; the same comings and goings of secondary characters; the same rudimentary psychology of the main characters; the same methods for endlessly eking out the public's favorite themes; the same ephemeral fashions; the same constant journeys being undertaken; the same crystallizations around a preposterous central figure (albeit, in this case, a virtuous and saintly one). And not only that: there is also the same daily-installment system. For just as today's reader is provided every morning with his daily dose, to which he hurriedly turns as soon as he is up, so, in those days, in convents and churches, at prime and matins, the faithful Christian was likewise provided with a daily installment of a *Passion* or a *Life* that dramatically sanctified his whole day, just as the daily toil of the present-day lower-class reader is given a dramatic halo by his morning's reading.

The denouements differ, of course. Or rather, our more practical age prefers to know that its tortured heroes have found a just compensation for their suffering in this life. In earlier times people were less demanding, and they were perfectly happy to think that, after so many trials and tribulations, the saint or martyr, after the final and decisive episode, had earned eternal felicity (weigh that word "eternal" well) in the company of the angels and his heroic predecessors. In short, the punishment of vice—in this case the unspeakable torments of hell—appeared to that Christian readership as something within the scope of its imagination, thanks to descriptions interpolated into sermons or, more directly, by means of a simple transference mechanism. It was in fact sufficient to accept that the physical torments inflicted on martyrs here below would be

meted out likewise to their tormentors, exactly repro-
duced, on that day when the malefactors finally descended
to the infernal regions—torments then not temporary but
eternal, incessantly inflicted, without truce or respite, to
eternal bodies. . . . It was a simple and consoling application of the old principle of an eye for an eye and a tooth for
a tooth. For if the torturer had spent an hour or two tearing
away at the saintly flesh of the martyr with red-hot pincers, was it not morally right that his own flesh should be
torn eternally by pincers that would glow red to the end of
time, since their heat was drawn from hell itself!

(*Religions, moeurs et légendes*, 3:150–51)

Nature and Sexuality

That throughout the entire biological series, from the most
primitive species up to the most highly evolved man, sexuality is the pole around which all impressions, all feelings,
all thoughts entwine is a totally self-evident fact. . . . In our
modern legal codes all sorts of vestiges persist from earlier
periods, when sexuality was regarded as the enemy; and it
is not without struggle that we are gradually rooting these
barbaric survivals out of our law codes.

In short, the progress of mankind consists in adapting
man to nature; and it is an odd fact that man is constantly
being diverted by the artificial, by his own inventions,
from the freedom in life that is his true aim.

. . . Thus, to the economic difficulties that already
present such obstacles to our full expansion, in a system of
civilization in which the distribution of wealth is in inverse
proportion to its production, we find added a scruple of
entirely human invention, a scruple that diminishes both
the receptive and expressive powers of those who suffer

from it. It is an observable fact that, except in cases of partial atrophy . . . any individual who exercises his sexual function normally enjoys much more highly developed sensations of sight, smell, hearing, taste, and touch and a resultingly profounder psychic life because the mechanism of irradiations is being brought into play.

Sexuality governs the plastic arts, music, literature, and, what is more, science.

("La Sexualité, fait naturel,"
La Psychologie et la vie 6 no. 8
[August 1932]: 210–11)

Hitler's Principle

It must be recognized that he [Hitler] possesses a supreme dexterity in juxtaposing contradictions and imposing on his "subjects" composite terms that, since they have no meaning, permit them to think anything. He reminds me of that celebrated ethnopsychologist Wilhelm Wundt, who, when he found it impossible to distinguish clearly between *Mythus* (myth) and *Märchen* (folktales), invented the terms *Mythusmärchen* and its opposite, *Märchenmythus*, which denote neither the one nor the other yet somehow denote both simultaneously while also distinguishing between them without actually doing so. Hitler must certainly have read Wundt. None of which, however, diminishes his personal magnetism, increases the intelligence of his followers, or decreases our obligation to regard his movement very seriously, if not with dread.

After which, perhaps, the Germans may find out what it means to be free.

(*Mercure de France*, 1 December
1933, p. 482)

The Dangers of Specialization
in Folklore

In devising the plan of my investigation, as well as in its
mode of presentation, I worked from the universal to the
particular, from the comparative and universal ethnographic approach to the strictly localized approach appropriate to the French or Alpine provincial monograph. In
other words, the successes already achieved are due to the
fact that, knowing almost all the inherent possibilities for
variation in transition rituals, seasonal ceremonies, saint
cults, hermit cults, and so on, and in the various magical
and religious rites, I was more likely to succeed in discerning possible dominants and variants, incompatibilities or
discrepancies, than someone who had been working from
the particular to the general. It is exactly comparable with
the case of a good specialist in surgery or medicine who
started off by spending ten or twelve years studying general medicine, as an intern, and only then began to
specialize in laryngology or gynecology. To start off specializing right away, as people tend to do today, hoping to
"catch up" on general medicine later, is a bad system.

So what I am really saying is that those who would like
to undertake similar investigations in their own district
would do well to begin by learning something about general ethnography, about national and comparative folklore,
and also to take courses in methodology and description. If
they don't, they will be unable to recognize their material
when they see it, just as I myself would be unable to recognize the important facts if I were entrusted with a
geological investigation, since geology is a science of which
I am completely ignorant.

("Contribution à la méthodologie
du folklore," pp. 33–34)

Ways and Customs of the
French Provinces

Ways and customs form part of the psychic armature and constitute the mental environment to which every individual unconsciously adapts, from the day of his birth and by virtue of inherited ancestral characteristics. From this point of view, one that has been established only gradually by the researches of ethnographers and folklorists of every country, ways and customs can no longer be regarded—as they still were a century ago—as mere oddities, as curiosities, or even as examples of degeneration. Rural life is not a poor imitation of middle-class or court life. On the contrary, it is from rural life that the middle classes, courtiers, our men of genius themselves, have all drawn their best energies, their power of feeling, their faculties of analysis and synthesis, in short their human value. This is clearly evident in our literature, and it explains why Corneille and Molière, Rabelais or Montaigne, Flaubert and Mistral, all have their own inimitable voices. And it is the blending of all these particularities from our villages and cantons, smelted together in the forge of Paris, that has made that city the storehouse of such various and yet unified intellectual currents.

(Unpublished notes
preserved in the Archives des arts
et traditions populaires)

French Wellerisms

Anyone who has read *The Pickwick Papers* will probably recall Mr. Pickwick's faithful servant, Sam Weller, as well as his worthy father. Now Sam Weller's manner of expressing himself is on occasion so idiosyncratic that folklorists, struggling to classify the world's proverbs and sayings, have assured him of added glory by giving his name to a particular category of expressions—expressions that are really neither quite proverbs nor yet quite maxims and that no one can quite see how to denote otherwise in Europe, although, if one were to look to the Moslem East for help, one might say that they are *hadiths*, which is to say opinions attributed to a real or supposed authority and transmitted by tradition in a set form.

It would be otiose to reproduce here all of Sam Weller's *hadiths*. . . . The first two we encounter when reading *The Pickwick Papers* will suffice. In chapter 10, when Sam Weller is in the process of cleaning the guests' boots at the inn and the little maid asks him to clean those of number 22 first, he objects: "No, no, 'Reg'lar rotation,' as Jack Ketch said wen he tied the men up." In chapter 12, toward the end, when Mr. Pickwick has sent for Sam Weller, in order to engage him as his servant, and tells him he will explain what is afoot: "That's it, sir," Sam Weller replies, " 'Out with it,' as the father said to the child wen it swallowed a farden." The process thus consists in formulating an obvious fact, a truism, or an idiotic remark so as to take shelter behind the authority of some personage, known or unknown, real or imaginary. Sam Weller's expressions may derive from hearsay or from reading; it may be that Dickens collected them at first hand from the common people. . . . There are wellerisms to be found even in Latin and Greek authors, in Plato for example: " 'The water will tell you,' said the guide to the traveler who asked if the river was deep." . . . But the odd fact is that Taylor was unable to find any—two or three very rare cases excepted—in France, Italy, Spain, or Portugal.

This is something I once pointed out in the *Mercure de*

France . . . and in fact the only one I was able to cite then was: "Oh, oh, he said in Portuguese." Taylor quotes my example and then adds: " 'Appetite comes with eating,' said Engest du Mans, 'and thirst with drinking' " (Rabelais, *Gargantua*), and " 'Mustn't spit in the must,' said old father Noah" (Balzac, *Les Paysans*). This last example was borrowed directly from the people by Balzac himself. . . . Since then, I have managed to note down a few more French wellerisms, as follows:

Heard in Nice while walking in the street: " 'Don't hit your fingers,' as the smith's wife used to tell her husband when he was hammering."

Collected in Ecurie, near Arras: an answer to someone asking for tobacco: " 'If you ain't got no tobacco, break your pipe,' as Jesus said to the disciples."

Same locality: " 'Two women pissing on the same dunghill means trouble ahead,' as old mother X said."

. . . I have found a possible example of the formation process in volume 1 of Alexandre Dumas's *Voyage en Suisse*. Six young men leave Martigny and are driven by a drunken coachman, who at every dangerous bend shouts over his shoulder: "Don't be 'feared, Napoleon came through 'ere!" From then on, every time some adventure befalls them, one or the other of the young men shouts out the same words: "Don't be 'feared, Napoleon came through 'ere!" And they all fall about, laughing at the allusion to their drunken coachman. Let us imagine those young men meeting again in Paris some years later; it will be enough for one of them to recall that droll journey and repeat the formula, with the addition of "As the Martigny coachman said," to provide us with a wellerism perfect in every respect.

That is a supposition, but I believe that it was in fact how things did happen in practice and that, in the majority of cases, all identification of the speaker quoted has become impossible.

(Mercure de France,
15 December 1933, pp. 700–704)

Van Gennep's Humor:
M A C L, or Epigraphy's Finest Hour

In the year 2211, as we know, the whole of Europe, pivoting upon the Ural mountains as though upon some gigantic hinge, sank 3,000 feet and vanished beneath the waves. Nothing of it remained visible but the mountainous masses of the Central Plateau, the Pyrenees, the Alps, the Carpathians, and a few isolated peaks.

The irruption of the waters took place during the night. It was so sudden that very few people succeeded in saving themselves by clambering up nearby slopes. Certain minor towns, villages, hamlets, and chalets did, however, survive, and their inhabitants continued for several centuries to display remarkable energy and a burning will to live. Eventually, indeed, states were constituted that developed an advanced civilization.

Yet the old instinct for struggle and rapine was not dead in the European Archipelago. There were wars and massacres, and by the end of the fourth millennium after Jesus Christ the European Archipelago had become totally depopulated.

The Asians, Africans, and Americans had quite enough to keep themselves fully occupied at home. They were gradually perfecting the legacy of scientific methods and technical inventions that Europe had bequeathed to them. And since they had plenty of fertile land and minerals to exploit, they could see no useful purpose during the next five or six thousand years in colonizing the Archipelago.

But the time eventually did come when the old familiar causes made emigration desirable. It was decided that the undertaking should be scientifically planned. In other words, geographers, topographers, and geometricians were assigned the task of dividing the islands up equitably into zones of influence; engineers studied the economic possibilities of the once more virgin land, and archeologists were made responsible for methodically exhuming whatever vestiges they could discover of a past whose vanished glory and former wealth were attested to by certain rare books and some hundreds of minor works preserved in the world's public libraries.

Heading one of the archeological expeditions was the celebrated T. D. B. Abdallah Sénoufo, professor of comparative epigraphy in the University of the United States of Chad. His previous forays abroad, and the sensational discoveries they had produced, marked him out as eminently suited for this responsible post. Moreover, his presence was absolutely essential at the digs themselves, for he was the only scientist in the world who could understand Ancient French and the various dialects of the former French provinces. Also, he possessed the only known copy of a linguistic atlas of the region, incomplete as a result of the cataclysm but all the more precious for that.

Lastly, Abdallah Sénoufo also had the advantage over his colleagues of knowing a little Latin, and it was to him that they owed the excellent translation into Neobagirmian of all the passages from Roman authors dealing with the geography and ethnography of the Alps.

The expedition took ship at the end of April 9040 and was soon approaching White Island, whose icy shores were bathed by the Rhodanian Sea. Despite gusty weather, the debarkation at various points in neighboring bays was accomplished without mishap. After a number of fruitless exploratory excavations, the expedition eventually set up camp at the foot of a hill, still unnamed at the time, which the patriotic archeologists soon took to calling Mount Chad.

A number of extremely ancient maps enabled them to establish that at one time, some seven thousand years earlier, this hill had risen above a small lake called Bourjé, or something rather like that.

From various indications that to the eye of an experienced archeologist left no room for doubt, it was established that the slopes of this hill had once been inhabited for a continuous period of two to three thousand years. Here and there it was possible to discern cavities, some round and some square. Methodically conducted excavations revealed forty-seven superimposed layers of debris and detritus in one of these cavities, each layer corresponding to a different civilization. The Bagirmians extricated every vital, telltale fragment with the greatest care, crated up their collection of potsherds, flints, and pieces of rusty iron, and then went on to explore each of the other cavities in turn.

One day in July the torrid heat and the glare off the sea obliged Professor Abdallah Sénoufo to seek shelter for a while. After a brief search he found a convenient cleft in the rock, containing a sort of natural seat. His head now shaded, a cool sea breeze playing on his face, the professor dozed off. But suddenly a bright beam of light struck one of his eyes, and the resultant sensation, perceived through the flesh of the eyelid, caused his eyes to reopen. About fifty yards away something was glittering—some metal object, beyond doubt.

The scientist selected a number of markers, such as branches and pebbles, then slowly advanced toward the shining object. One must have had personal experience of archeology to understand the shock of joy that transfixed

Professor Abdallah Sénoufo at that moment: the object was a thin brass plaque, worn through in places, badly eroded in others, and extensively patinated except for the very center, which had remained quite clean and on which could be discerned a kind of plump face. In one corner there could also be seen the vestiges, albeit very worn, of a number of letters.

Having first delicately wrapped the plaque in his handkerchief, the professor summoned his staff, had the area cleared, and began systematic excavations. It became clear that the site must have been that of a dwelling, but no further interesting remains came to light. Since scientific method has proved fruitless, Abdallah Sénoufo thought to himself, let us put our faith in blind chance. And as it turned out, several days later, 204 feet, 8¾ inches from the first find he stubbed his toes against a second brass plaque, thinner than the first, without a central figure, but bearing four capital letters in relief. Excavations were continued until the onset of winter; the professor ventured forth on innumerable walks, but nothing further of interest was found. The expedition therefore returned to Sipar, the capital of the United States of Chad, and the professor settled down to write his report.

Since this report, which takes up seventy-two folio volumes of small print with diagrams, plans, maps, and explanatory notes, is to be found in every public and private library, I shall leave the reader to consult it himself on the broader issues, contenting myself here with a brief summary of volumes 37–58, which are specifically devoted to an examination of the two brass plaques.

As to the first, Abdallah Sénoufo's interpretations must be accepted totally and without reservation. It is perfectly evident that the central figure represents the plump face of an adolescent and that the lines radiating from the face and extending almost as far as the raised border, portions of which still remain around the edge of the plaque, are *sunbeams*.

Confirmation of this idea is provided by the fact that in the top right-hand corner it is possible to make out the letters EIL. Since the learned professor has been at pains to draw up a list of all the very ancient French words that ended in EIL, we are in a position to conclude that the words OEIL, CONSEIL, and others like them offer no meaning that has any relation to the central image and that the word SOLEIL alone—in our language SUN—corresponds to the representation of the plump face surrounded by rays. The plaque is unfortunately too worn for it to be possible to reconstruct the words that very probably preceded the final SOLEIL.

Whatever they may have been, however, it remains certain that this piece of evidence throws a clear light on the mentality of the former denizens of Mount Chad. One may even say that we are at last in a position to establish their religion. For there can be no doubt that a material as valuable as brass could only have served to honor their divinities. From this it naturally follows that the plaque in question can be nothing other than a very ancient votive plaque, dedicated by a number of Frenchmen to the Sun God, probably to ensure that he would ripen—or to thank him for having ripened—their crops.

Professor Sénoufo justifiably recalls in this context that an author too much neglected today, for he was one our most worthy predecessors, a certain Georges Cumont, had observed the wide diffusion of sun worship in Europe toward the end of the first millennium after Jesus Christ.

This worship must have persisted over several centuries, and it certainly flourished in the fertile regions around Mount Chad, formerly known as *Savoy*, toward the end of the second millennium after Jesus Christ. It is difficult, when dealing with such distant times, to achieve absolute precision. Give or take a few centuries, sun worship must therefore have continued in the region of ancient Europe for about fifteen hundred to three thousand years.

It is to the same period of civilization that the second object discovered ought likewise to be assigned. Thanks to delicate but industrious scouring, Professor Abdallah Sénoufo succeeded in establishing that the four letters worked in relief on the plaque were M A C L.

Since epigraphy is his specialty, he underwent long hesitations in deciphering and dating them. Epigraphically speaking, these letters belong to the noble script known as Monumental Latin. The earliest examples of it occur about halfway through the first millennium before Jesus Christ, and it remained in use until the cataclysm of 2211. It will be seen, therefore, that there is a perfect concordance between the two plaques.

The first idea that occurred to the professor was that this second plaque, like the first, was a Latin-French *ex-voto*. Some of the region's gods are known to us, and among them we find MERCURIUS, CARLOMAG(NUS), NAPOLEO(N), and LIVAROT. This last is known to us solely from a fragment of a wooden container discovered on a peak of Auvergne Island by the Japanese expedition of several years ago and miraculously preserved beneath a layer of volcanic ash. Since no other mention of the god LIVAROT (the spelling is indisputable) has been encountered in the Alpine Archipelago, we believe, with Professor Sénoufo, that there are no grounds for entertaining the above hypothesis further.

It would take too long to examine all the theories, some of them extremely attractive, successively put forward by the ingenious epigraphist. There is a great temptation, for example, to link this mysterious word with the name of another divinity, possibly female, of which it might be viewed as an abbreviation for the use of initiates in her sacred mysteries. The complete name of this divinity was IMAKULEKONSEPSION, which initiates may well have abbreviated to MACL in their prayers. The difference in spelling is not in fact as important as laymen might suppose, in view of the fact that the goddess's complete name is known only from a piece of slate for the use of children during their period of initiation into the mysteries, upon which they inscribed what I shall make so bold as to call their "lessons." The amended spelling would thus be IMACLECON-SEΨIΩN.

For very weighty reasons, however, our celebrated compatriot rejects this interpretation, along with the following, which did at least have the merit of putting him on the right track: we know that among Americans descended from primitive European settlers there are still a few rare families whose surname begins with *Mac*.

Professor Sénoufo has even succeeded in drawing up a very curious list of these family names, such as Macfarlane, Maclean (the name of an ancient king famous for his beautiful teeth), Macgillicuddy, and others of the same sort. It is unclear, however, why a name of this kind should have been partially raised in relief on a precious brass plaque, especially in view of the fact that such names were invariably localized in Scotchisland. But the idea that MACL might possess an ethnographic significance was a fertile one.

The proof of this is that Professor Abdallah Sénoufo solved the problem with an elegance that leaves nothing to be desired. A thorough combing of all the extremely ancient books still in existence on the peoples who colonized the Alpine region, in which Mount Chad is situated, produced a list of four tribes whose initial letters correspond

exactly with those that figure on the plaque. Here they are:
M EDULLES; A LLOBROGES; C EUTRONS; L IGURES.

The plaque in question is therefore clearly the token of
an alliance concluded by those four peoples in the course
of the first millennium after Jesus Christ and perhaps,
given the proximity of the two discovery sites, involving an
invocation to the sun god. The discovery of this historical
fact is beyond doubt of incalculable importance. It throws a
dazzling light upon that distant past, and it is with pride
that we once again salute our illustrious fellow countryman
as one of the torchbearers of archeological science.

Let me finish this account, at times somewhat arid, on a
humorous note. Professor Abdallah Sénoufo is by now a
great-grandfather. Among his grandchildren there is one,
Omar, now thirty-three years old, who in his youth
learned the ancient French language with his grandfather's
help and now promises to be a worthy successor to him
when the day of the venerable Abdallah's retirement eventually dawns. One day, at dinner, this young man announced that he thought he understood the inscription
that was costing his grandfather such labors and so many
late nights at that time:

"You know, grandpa," he said, "I'm quite sure that in
ancient French MACL meant MAISON ASSURÉE CONTRE
L'INCENDIE"—which in our language signifies: house in-
sured against fire."

The professor was indulgence itself, and, instead of rep-
rimanding his grandson with the severity he deserved, the
kindly old man began to chuckle, then to laugh, then to
shake and roar with mirth until he seemed about to burst.

"Oh, my child—for I can no longer say 'my pupil,'" he
managed to get out at last, "don't you see that your
exegesis is founded upon an epigraphic impossibility!"

(*Les Demi-savants*, pp. 115–33)

NOTES

CHAPTER ONE

1. A brief biography prefaces the bibliography of his works compiled by his daughter.

2. After Marillier's death in 1901, he was succeeded by Marcel Mauss, who was followed in 1940 by Maurice Leenhardt. The post has been occupied since 1951 by Claude Lévi-Strauss, who has renamed it the "Chair of Compared Religions of Peoples without Writing." Marcel Mauss was appointed to this post at the Ecole pratique (where he had risen from lecturer to assistant director and then finally to director of studies) at a very early age, for he was only twenty-nine. Born in 1872, he was an almost exact contemporary of Van Gennep.

3. Van Gennep's notes and manuscripts are preserved in the Musée des arts et traditions populaires. I wish to express my heartfelt thanks to its chief curator, M. Jean Cuisenier, for having allowed me access to its archives, and also to Mme Geneviève Veyssière for her help with my work there.

4. "Folklore et culture vivante," in *Le livre blanc de l'ethnocide en Amérique*, edited by R. Jaulin (Paris: Fayard, 1972), p. 359.

5. Claude Lévi-Strauss, "Le Père Noël supplicié," *Les Temps modernes*, no. 77 (1952), p. 1584.

CHAPTER TWO

1. Claude Lévi-Strauss, *Le Totémisme aujourd'hui* (Paris: Presses Universitaires de France, 1962), p. 6.

2. The subtitle of *L'Etat actuel du problème totémique* is very revealing in this respect: *Etude critique des théories sur les origines de la religion et de l'organisation sociale*.

CHAPTER SIX

1. It was Van Gennep who had translated Havelock Ellis's *Studies in Sexual Psychology* into French during the years 1912–35.

2. *Dictionnaire encyclopédique des sciences du langage* (Paris: Seuil, 1972), article "Synchronie et diachronie."

3. Claude Lévi-Strauss, "Les champignons dans la culture," *L'Homme* 10, no. 1 (1970): 12.

CHAPTER SEVEN

1. In 1906 he was forced to postpone publication because of the sheer magnitude of the material to be processed and also because of difficulties over the hundreds of illustrative plates needed (*Religions, moeurs et légendes*, 2:257).

CHAPTER EIGHT

1. It is worth noting that Van Gennep occupied himself a great deal with folk cults to saints. A great many articles—too many to be cited here—bear witness to this.

2. Claude Lévi-Strauss, "Ce que l'ethnologie doit à Durkheim," *Annales de l'Université de Paris*, no. 1 (1960), pp. 47–52.

BIBLIOGRAPHY

A bibliography of Van Gennep's works has been compiled and published by his daughter Ketty. Although very full, it is still not exhaustive. The book reviews and analyses are listed only with the name of the publication in which they appeared, the date, and the page numbers. This bibliography is preceded by a short biography and concludes with four indexes: of proper names, geographical names, subjects, and names of periodicals.

K. Van Gennep. *Bibliographie des oeuvres d'Arnold Van Gennep*. Preface by G.-H. Rivière. Paris: A. and J. Picard, 1964. 93 pp.

Van Gennep himself compiled a much more detailed bibliography at the time of his candidacy for the Collège de France. This goes only up to 1911, however.

Notices des titres et travaux scientifiques de M. A. Van Gennep. Paris: Ch. Renaudie, 1911.

Below I list all of Van Gennep's most important works. Most are out of print but can be found in libraries.

1904

Tabou et totémisme à Madagascar: Etude descriptive et théorique (Taboo and Totemism in Madagascar: A Descriptive and Theoretical Study). Paris: Leroux. 363 pp. (No. 17 of the series Bibliothèques des Hautes Etudes, sciences religieuses.)

This was a diploma thesis written at the Ecole des Hautes Etudes under the partial supervision of Léon Marillier, who lectured there on "Religions of Noncivilized Peoples" (see note referred to on p. 3).

1906

Mythes et légendes d'Australie: Etude d'ethnographie et de sociologie (Myths and Legends of Australia: An Ethnographic and Sociological Study). Paris: Guilmoto. cxvi + 183 pp.

1908–14

Religions, moeurs et légendes: Essais d'ethnographie et linguistique (Religions, Ways, and Legends: Ethnographic and Linguistic Essays). 5 vols. Paris: Mercure de France.

Van Gennep collected in these five volumes (which appeared in 1908, 1909, 1911, 1912, and 1914) what he considered the most important of his articles that had previously been published in various periodicals. They enable us to appreciate a particularly engaging aspect of his scientific personality: his extremely lively curiosity, his gifts of observation, his taste for polemic, and the breadth of his culture.

1909

Les Rites de passage (Rites of Passage). Paris: Nourry. 288 pp.

This epoch-making book was republished jointly by Johnson Reprint and Mouton in 1969 in a facsimile edition (no. 5 in the series Maison des Sciences de l'Homme Rééditions). The publishers also had the happy notion of appending the corrections inked or penciled in by Van Gennep in his own personal copy.

1910
La Formation des légendes (The Formation of Legends). Paris: Flammarion. 326 pp. 2d ed., 1922.

1911
"Etudes d'ethnographie algérienne" (Studies in Algerian Ethnography). *Revue d'ethnographie et de sociologie*, vol. 2. 112 pp.

1911
Les Demi-savants (Pseudo-Scientists). Paris: Mercure de France. 210 pp.

1914
En Algérie (In Algeria). Paris: Mercure de France. 220 pp.

1916
En Savoie (In Savoy). Vol. 1: *Du Berceau à la tombe* (From Cradle to Grave). Chambéry: Dardel. 328 pp.

A second volume, to be entitled *From New Year's Day to Christmas*, never appeared.

1920
L'Etat actuel du problème totémique: Etude critique des théories sur les origines de la religion et de l'organisation sociale (The Present State of the Totemic Problem: A Critical Study of

Theories on the Origins of Religion and Social Organization). Paris: Leroux. 363 pp.

This book appeared first in the form of articles in the *Revue de l'histoire des religions* 75:295–370; 76:281–347; 79:14–74; 80:86–153 and 193–270. It was Van Gennep's thesis for his doctorate of letters.

1922

Traité comparatif des nationalités (Comparative Treatise on Nationalities). Vol. 1: *Les Eléments extérieurs des nationalités* (The External Elements of Nationality). Paris: Payot. 228 pp.

The treatise was to have comprised two further volumes that never appeared: vol. 2, *La Formation de la nationalité*, and vol. 3, *La Vie des nationalités* (The Formation of Nationality and The Life of Nationalities).

1924

Le Folklore: Croyances et coutumes populaires françaises. (Folklore: French Folk Beliefs and Customs). Paris: Stock. 128 pp. (No. 11 of the series La Culture moderne).

1932–33

Le Folklore du Dauphiné (Isère): Etude descriptive et comparée de psychologie populaire (The Folklore of the Dauphiné [Isère]: A Descriptive and Comparative Study of Folk Psychology). 2 vols. Paris: Maisonneuve. 792 pp. (Nos. 2 and 3 of the series Les Littératures populaires de toutes les nations.)

These two works inaugurated the series of major monographs on French folklore deriving from Van Gennep's own firsthand investigations, from the questionnaires he sent out to his correspondents, or from both methods in combination. There were five more, as follows:

1934

Le Folklore de la Bourgogne (Côte d'Or), avec une discussion théorique sur le prétendu culte des sources (The Folklore of Burgundy [Côte d'Or], with a Theoretical Discussion of So-called Well and Spring Worship). Paris: Maisonneuve. 254 pp. (No. 1 of the series Contributions au folklore des provinces de France.)

The series Contributions to the Folklore of the French Provinces was launched by Van Gennep himself. It includes a number of excellent monographs on the folklore of a number of French regions. This same year saw the publication of an important article on folklore methods that enables us to assess the development in Van Gennep's ideas during the ten years since *Le Folklore* of 1924:

1934

"Contribution à la méthodologie du folklore" (Contribution to the Methodology of Folklore). *Lares*, vol. 5, no. 1, pp. 20–34.

1935

Le Folklore de la Flandre et du Hainaut français (département du Nord) (The Folklore of Flanders and French Hainaut). 2 vols. Paris: Maisonneuve. 737 pp. (Nos. 2 and 3 of Contributions au folklore des provinces de France.)

Both of these monographs published in 1934 and 1935 included an appendix. The 1934 appendix was entitled "Etude sur la répartition géographique des géants processionels" (Study on the Geographical Distribution of

Processional Giants), that in the 1935 work "Contribution à la théorie générale des patronages" (A Contribution to the General Theory of Guilds).

1942
Le Folklore de l'Auvergne et du Velay (The Folklore of the Auvergne and Velay). Paris: Maisonneuve. 375 pp. (No. 5 of Contributions au folklore des provinces de France.)

1946
Le Folklore des Hautes-Alpes: Etude descriptive et comparée de psychologie populaire (The Folklore of the Hautes-Alpes: A Descriptive and Comparative Study in Folk Psychology). 2 vols. Paris: Maisonneuve. 432, 321 pp. (No. 9 [n.s.] in Les Littératures populaires de toutes les nations.)

1938–58
Manuel de folklore français contemporain (A Manual of Contemporary French Folklore). Paris: Picard.

Vol. 1, pt. 1 (1943). *Introduction générale. Du Berceau à la tombe: Naissance, baptême, enfance, adolescence, fiançailles* (General Introduction. From Cradle to Grave: Birth, Baptism, Childhood, Adolescence, Betrothal). 373 pp.

Vol. 1, pt. 2 (1946). *Du Berceau à la tombe (fin): Mariage, funérailles* (From Cradle to Grave [Conclusion]: Marriage, Funerals). Pp. 373–830.

Vol. 1, pt. 3 (1947). *Cérémonies périodiques cycliques. 1: Carnaval, Carême, Pâques* (Seasonal Cyclic Ceremonies. 1: Shrove Tuesday, Lent, Easter). Pp. 833–1416.

Vol. 1, pt. 4 (1949). *Cérémonies périodiques cycliques. 2: Cycle de mai, la Saint-Jean* (Seasonal Cyclic Ceremonies. 2: The May Cycle, Midsummer's Day). Pp. 1421–2135.

Vol. 1, pt. 5 (1951). *3: Les Cérémonies agricoles et pastorales de l'été* (Summer Agricultural and Pastoral Ceremonies). Pp. 2137–2543.

Vol. 1, pt. 6 (1953). *4: Les Cérémonies agricole et pastorales de l'automne* (Autumn Agricultural and Pastoral Ceremonies). Pp. 2545–2854.

Vol. 1, pt. 7 (1958). *Cycle des Douze Jours* (The Twelve Days of Christmas Cycle). Pp. 2855–3166. (Published posthumously.)

Vol. 3 (1937). *Questionnaires. Provinces et pays. Bibliographie méthodique* (Questionnaires. Provinces and Districts. Systematic Bibliography). 552 pp.

Vol. 4 (1938). *Bibliographie méthodique (fin). Index.* (Systematic Bibliography [Conclusion]. Index). Pp. 533–1078.

The various parts of the *Manuel* have been listed systematically rather than chronologically in order to demonstrate the general plan of the work more clearly.

Van Gennep's fragmentary notes for the conclusion of his *Manuel*, several passages from which I have quoted, will appear, thanks to the good offices of M. Jean Cuisenier, Head Curator of the Musée des arts et traditions populaires, in a forthcoming number of *Archives d'ethnologie française* (Paris: Maisonneuve & Larose).

INDEX